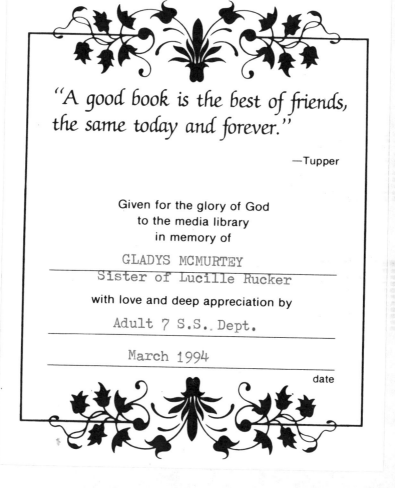

"A good book is the best of friends, the same today and forever."

—Tupper

Given for the glory of God
to the media library
in memory of

GLADYS MCMURTEY

Sister of Lucille Rucker

with love and deep appreciation by

Adult 7 S.S. Dept.

March 1994

date

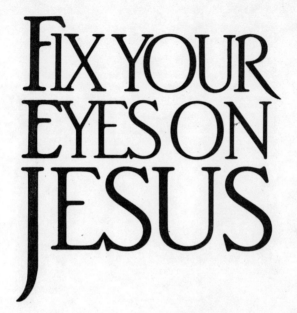

FIX YOUR EYES ON JESUS

ANNE ORTLUND

4652

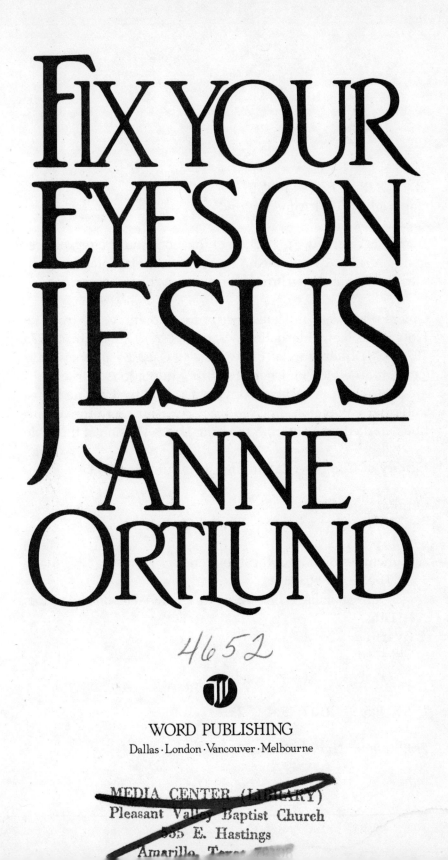

WORD PUBLISHING
Dallas · London · Vancouver · Melbourne

FIX YOUR EYES ON JESUS
Copyright © 1991 Anne Ortlund

Unless otherwise indicated, Scripture quotations are from the Holy Bible, New International Version (NIV). Copyright © 1973, 1978, 1984 International Bible Society. Used by permission of Zondervan Bible Publishers. Scripture quotations marked (TLB) are from The Living Bible, copyright © 1971 by Tyndale House Publishers, Wheaton, Il. Used by permission. Scripture quotations marked (KJV) are from the King James Version of the Bible.

Library of Congress Cataloging-in-Publication Data

Ortlund, Anne.
    Fix your eyes on Jesus / by Anne Ortlund.
      p.   cm.
    Includes bibliographical references.
    ISBN 0-8499-0856-6
    1. Christian life—1960- 2. Jesus Christ—Person and offices.
I. Title.
BV4501.2.0726 1991
248.4—dc20   91-4329
                                              CIP

1 2 3 4 5 9 RRD 5 4 3 2 1

Printed in the United States of America

To Ray
husband
lover
coach
model
shaper
cheering section
pastor
leader
inspirer
confidante
counselor
playmate
best friend
co-laborer in the gospel
one whose very life urges me to fix my eyes on Jesus

CONTENTS

I was chatting last Sunday with my in-laws; they're dear people. We covered this and that, and got to discussing a particular pastor. Oh, so subtly, so delicately, I managed to allude to his struggles, perils, possible problems. . . . I rattled on. . . .

Suddenly I saw myself—fangs, claws, and all.

I was making sure they understood that Ray and I had never had such struggles, perils, possible problems—that we must obviously be superior. . . . I was too well-bred to say it; I only inferred it. My relatives are savvy people; they'd understand.

The Spirit stopped me cold.

My eyes weren't on Jesus, they were on my family—to make sure Ray and I looked good in their sight. That gave freedom to my "old nature" (my familiar, ugly, life-long enemy) to take control of my tongue, and there in front of all of them was my exposed heart, with all its lurking pride and jealousy.

Embarrassing! Discouraging!

I apologized, and my sweet family made light of it and of course forgave me.

But I'm always just one step from disaster, aren't you? And there's no help, no winning, unless we follow Hebrews 12:2— fix our eyes on Jesus, one moment at a time.

Do you need this book? I do. Let's learn from it and obey what it says together.

Fix your eyes on Jesus as your Example, and be ashamed.
Fix your eyes on Jesus as your Savior, and be rescued.
Fix your eyes on Jesus as your Physician, and be made whole.
Fix your eyes on Jesus as your Mentor, and be taught.
Fix your eyes on Jesus as your Comforter, and be encouraged.
Fix your eyes on Jesus as your Strength, and be enabled.
Fix your eyes on Jesus as your Life, and live abundantly forever.

"Look . . . and live"
(Numbers 21:8)

There was a time when the Israelites in the desert had gotten into so much sin that God sent snakes among them to bite them, and many died. But then God said to Moses,

"Make a snake and put it up on a pole; anyone who is bitten can look at it and live." So Moses made a bronze snake and put it up on a pole. Then when anyone was bitten by a snake and looked at the bronze snake, he lived (Numbers 21:8–9).

And Jesus — the final, ultimate Healer — told Nicodemus,

Just as Moses lifted up the snake in the desert, so the Son of Man must be lifted up, that everyone who believes in him may have eternal life (John 3:14–15).

But does Jesus, lifted up, seem too remote? Or does He intimidate you? I'm praying as I write that you'll understand just how personable He is.

"Come to me," He says (Matthew 11:28).

"Handle me, and see" (Luke 24:39, KJV).

How tender He is, how unthreatening! He's wooing you, saying, "Don't be afraid; just believe" (Mark 5:36).

> He does not fight or shout;
> He does not raise His voice!
> He does not crush the weak
> or quench the smallest hope (Matthew 12:19, TLB).

God is on one side and all the people on the other side, and Christ Jesus, himself man, is between them to bring them together

(1 Timothy 2:5, TLB).

So come, my friend. *I* came many years ago. You come, too.

Let us draw near with a true heart, in absolute assurance of faith, our hearts sprinkled clean from a bad conscience (Hebrews 10:22, Moffatt). For Christ . . . suffered for sins, the just for the unjust, that he might bring us to God (1 Peter 3:18, KJV).

For your personal salvation, what an "unspeakable gift" He is (2 Corinthians 9:15)! — or as the Living Bible says, a "Gift too wonderful for words."

Fix your eyes on Jesus.

*There is no beauty to be discovered anywhere
comparable to fixing your eyes on Jesus.
There is no life-changing power available anywhere
comparable to that gaze.*

2

"Look to Me"
(Isaiah 45:22)

I crawled into bed last night thinking about Ray's news, that a fellow's going to do a few guest-speaker spots on Ray's *Haven of Rest* broadcast. Ray was still in the bathroom, but I called in loudly to him, "Did you tell him it's to renew and encourage believers? We don't want somebody ranting and raving over social issues and controversies. Does he understand *Haven's* flavor?"

Ray came around the corner and got into bed. "Don't be such a fusser, Anne. Why are you fussing?"

We hugged each other and I bellowed in his ear, "What do you mean, fuss? I never fuss! It's totally contrary to my gentle, mellow nature to fuss!" And we laughed ourselves silly. (It's great living together after the kids are gone. You can scream and yell and do what you want.)

Of course we both knew my natural inclination *is* to fuss. I'm conscientious and meticulous and I'm always anticipating how to cover details. Though I've been a Christian for many years, I can still fuss; I can be really obnoxious. Then it's back to repenting and refocusing my eyes on Jesus — and I'm once more relaxed and happy.

You see, the Lord says to you and me continually,

> Look unto me, and be ye saved . . .
> For I am God,
>   and there is none else (Isaiah 45:22, KJV).

I need constantly to be saved *from myself.* Do you? Do you need to be saved from
> your fears,
> your angers,
> your bad memories,
> your orneryness,
> your addictions,
> your temptations to escape instead of to conquer,
> your lusts,
> your depressions,
> your laziness?

Says Hebrews 12:2, *"Fix your eyes on Jesus."*

> Maybe you're more absorbed in looking at *people,* to save you from yourself.
> But God says,
>
> > "Man . . . is of few days and full of trouble. . . .
> >   Like a fleeting shadow, he does not endure.
> > Do you fix your eyes on such a one?" (Job 14:1–3).
>
> No, no, we mustn't.
> "Lord," said Peter, "to whom else shall we go? You have the words of eternal life" (John 6:68).

Listen:

> Whether you aren't yet a Christian,
> Or you're a new one,
> Or you've walked with Him a long time—

*The only eternal, universal, triumphant, ever-contemporary Lord Jesus Christ (the One with the scars in His hands) commands, "Give Me your full attention. I Myself, and I only, hold the answers for every circumstance of your life. **Fix your eyes on Me.**"*

It's the look that saves, but it's the gaze that sanctifies.

PART 1

Fix your eyes on Jesus
to get practical help

"What does it take," someone asked a circus tightrope walker, "to do what you do?"

"Three things," he answered.

"*Raw courage*. You commit yourself to begin walking, and then you can't change your mind.

"*Balance*. You can't lean too far this way or that.

"Most of all, *concentration*. You fix your eyes on that wire, and until it's all over you never shift your attention."

He paused. Then—

"Never," he said firmly.

3

Fix your eyes on Jesus
when you feel without direction

A radio psychologist in our area has a daily call-in show. Recently I happened to flip the dial, and this is what I heard:

"Doctor, I can't seem to stick with anything. I've had three marriages; before long each of them bored me. People say I have talents, but I go from one job to another; I don't seem to be able to hang in there."

"You know what's missing?"

"No, what?"

"Passion!"

"I started to get a college degree, but I ran out of money so I couldn't finish. . . . "

"Nothing consumes you. Your life doesn't have any forward-moving energy."

"I started painting for a hobby once, but it took an awful lot of time, and I don't know. . . . "

"Listen to me, pal, listen to me: what do you burn to do?"

For some reason at that moment I thought of sheep.

You know how a sheep is. He keeps his head down and goes nibble, nibble, nibble.

Out of the corner of his eye he sees a new tuft of grass; he moves four inches right . . . nibble, nibble.

Then out of the corner of his eye he sees another tuft; he moves six inches left . . . nibble, nibble.

When have you seen a sheep climb a tree, check the horizons, see where he's come from and where he wants to go, and climb down and strike out? Never.

(No wonder Isaiah 53:6 says, "All we like sheep have gone astray. . . .")

Are you identifying with a sheep? *Do you pretty much live with your head down?*

Now it's time to go to work . . .

Mustn't forget to pick up the pants at the cleaners . . .

It's five o'clock; wonder what I should fix for dinner . . .

It's Thursday and my book's due back to the library . . .

It's five minutes till time for the school bus . . .

Nibble, nibble, nibble . . . ?

What consumes you? Where are you going? Have you pinpointed your aim? Does your life have a specific target?

You know, deep inside, what you need.

Fix your eyes on Jesus.

Whatever your lifestye, your situation, your connections— first of all, most of all, fix your eyes on Him. *Dedicate yourself to make Him your focus. Let all your other loves flow out of that.*

You'll grow downward and upward and outward—but you'll always be stable, centralized, focused, balanced.

("Balance," the circus tightrope walker said. "You can't lean too far this way or that.")

Jesus Himself

strengthens your weaknesses,

tones down your excesses,

brings your under-normals up to normal and makes your
above-normals not seem over-powering and intimidating,
refines what is crude,
helps the rigid to relax,
helps the over-polished to loosen up,
helps the lowly born to get "class."

Some people don't want to fix their eyes on Jesus; they
imagine that would make them religious freaks. Listen:

> *Jesus Christ is the only One Who is perfectly whole and
> healthy and balanced and normal. And the more you fix your
> eyes on Him, the more whole and healthy and balanced and nor-
> mal you will be.*

> *Fix your eyes on Jesus.*

Why don't you pray to Him something like this:

Lord Jesus Christ, it's time for me to get more turned to
Your direction. I want this to be a new-beginning time in
my life.
I want to learn to fix my eyes on You. Help me as I read this
book. And show me how to make it practical and real in
my life—tailor-made for me.
I love You, Lord! In Your holy name, amen.

4

Fix your eyes on Jesus
when you have too much to do

Ten months after Ray and I were married we had baby Sherry.

Eleven and a half months later we had Margie.

Seventeen months later we had Buddy.

And immediately after that, Ray had a shrew for a wife.

My problem wasn't Ray or the babies; all four were adorable! My problem was no quiet time, no focus. My eyes weren't fixed on Jesus, they were fixed on what I had to do.

A work-centered life gets complex, and it leads to burnout. A Christ-centered life—even in the midst of work—stays basically simple, nourished, and rested.

(When I got ornery enough to get desperate, I got back to Jesus again. Then little by little I didn't yell so much, and I guess Ray decided he could stick out being married to me after all.)

Learn from two of my weak areas:

One, especially in earlier days, sometimes *I wasn't really as busy as I felt I was busy.* The pressure I put on myself kept "overheating my motor" and making me feel pushed.

Two, *I tended to feel crowded periods before they ever arrived,* and to be tired just from anticipating them.

You see, *our actual living is between our ears.* If you're unhappy or anxious over what's happening or what's going to happen, that's what tenses your muscles and starts to erode you.

Then *don't fix your eyes on what you have to do.* When I've done that it's made me fragmented and harried.

> "Martha, Martha," the Lord said, "you are worried and upset about many things, but only one thing is needed. Mary has chosen what is better" (Luke 10:41–42).

Martha's problem wasn't cooking, it was the "many things." She was multi-directional, which always makes us oppressed, nervous, burdened, self-pitying, off-balance.

> When your eyes are on Him, you begin to develop a reflex action inside you—it may take time—that shuns what's complicating, what's overwhelming. You'll find you want to *do less* (but do the most important things) to *become more.*
>
> Although truly, the more you become, the more you actually achieve. And then your life begins to have wider-ranging and longer-lasting effects.

Fix your eyes on Jesus! Like Mary, focus; that's what I had to learn. Become a "one-thing" person (Luke 10:42).

How do you do this?

First, begin to develop the habit of continual fellowship with Him (see chapter 18) in the midst of it all.

Second, determine to give Him the sacrifice of a regular "quiet time" (see chapter 19). Yes, it will be a true sacrifice. ("You will never *find time* for anything," says Charles Bixton. "If you want time you must *make* it.")

Third, give Him frequent spaces when you momentarily quit, relax, breathe deeply, stretch your body, and say, "Jesus, my eyes are on You. You are able. You are helping me from one moment to the next. I trust You."

As you seek to do those three things and release control to Him, He will

> make the hours stretch,
> bring others to help you,
> cancel some things you thought you had to do,
> show you duties you can delegate,
> show you duties which don't have to be done at all.

I didn't learn my lessons once for all. I've had to come back over and over to take seriously again His practical words,

> Reverence for God adds hours to each day (Proverbs 10:27, TLB).

Let's pray to Him—you and I, Anne Ortlund—together:

Lord Jesus, according to Matthew 11:29, we take Your yoke upon us. We want to learn from You—Creator, Producer, Worker, Achiever! Be our Model, and teach us Your rhythm for living, so that as we live, we'll find rest for our souls. In Your dear name, amen.

For the weariest day
May Christ be thy stay.
For the darkest night
May Christ be thy light.
For the weakest hour
May Christ be thy power.
For each moment's fall
May Christ be thy all.
　　　　—Old benediction

5

Fix your eyes on Jesus
when you're lonely

Have you moved recently and lost friends and you're lonely?

Or have your friends moved and lost *you*, and you're lonely?

Or do you have people all around but they don't know you well, or worse, don't understand you—and you're lonely?

Or are you a shut-in, and you're lonely?

Fix your eyes on the only One Who truly understands, because He's the only One Who has ever experienced true loneliness.

Jesus wasn't totally lonely when His own family thought He was crazy (Mark 3:21).

He wasn't totally lonely when all the people of His own hometown tried to kill Him (Luke 4:28–29).

He wasn't totally lonely
> when His own fellow nationals took the responsibility
> for having Him crucified (Matthew 27:24–25),
> or when one of His very own disciples turned Him in to
> make it happen (Matthew 26:14–16),

28

or when His much-loved Peter denied any connection
with Him (John 18:25–27),
or even when eventually every one of His eleven best
friends left Him in the lurch (Matthew 26:56).
Through it all He could turn to His Father for much-needed
comfort and fellowship.

*But then, for the first time in eternity, Jesus discovered true, ul-
timate loneliness.* When He "became sin for us" (2 Corinthians
5:21), God Himself had to turn His face away and cut Him off.
Suddenly Jesus had no one at all—not even God!
In this new, strange, hellish horror, Jesus let loose a roar: "My
God, my God, why have you forsaken me?" (Matthew 27:46).

[It is] a scream of despairing agony in the darkness. It is the
picture of an eclipsed God and a lost soul; it is the hour and
power of darkness: the hosts of hell fill it, and the opaque sins
of a world thicken it: It is Jesus bearing MY sin in His own
body on the tree. It is Jesus taking the place of a lost soul.[1]

*Jesus on the cross became truly lonely, so that you and I would
never need to be.*

Listen carefully:
Your loneliness is unnecessary.
Do you know that?
In fact, if loneliness is long-term and chronic with you, *it's
disobedient.* It's not taking seriously His promise, "Surely I will
be with you always" (Matthew 28:20).
You see,

---

*When on the cross Jesus found out what real loneliness
felt like, He made sure it need never happen to you.*

---

[1] Oswald J. Sanders, *Christ Incomparable*, p. 167.

This is your secret to overcoming loneliness: *Fix your eyes on Him.* People suggest lots of prescriptions: get busy, get involved in your church and community, do things for others, find a friend, join a small group—no, no! Not first!

First in your loneliness, *draw from Jesus.* See how He drew and drew from His Father, His ever-flowing Source of all love and comfort and hope and pleasure and fullness:

> Very early in the morning, when it was still dark, Jesus got up . . . and prayed (Mark 1:35).

He even deliberately *sought aloneness,* for the best togetherness of all:

> Crowds of people came to hear him . . . but Jesus often withdrew to lonely places and prayed (Luke 5:15–16).

You do the same. Sit at His feet, and spread out your loneliness before Him. Apologize! Admit you've been fixing your eyes on yourself—no wonder.

He is complete in the Father, and He says you are complete in Him (Colossians 2:9–10). He—and only He—*is full of fullness for you.* When, humanly speaking, you feel all alone, your heart can still be happy and satisfied: *You are complete in Him.*

> Though my father and mother forsake me,
> the Lord will receive me (Psalm 27:10).

Read the Bible; feast on it. Jesus is "Immanuel—God with you" (Matthew 1:23). He is closer than close, tender, comforting. *He loves you!* Drink in all that He is; He will become in you "a spring of water welling up to everlasting life" (John 4:14; 7:38).

Then in that fullness, go to touch other lives: Get involved in your church and community, do things for others, find a friend, join a small group. . . .[2]

Wherever you go, you'll go in the spirit of satisfaction and wholeness and deep-welling joy—because *first you were healed; first you fixed your eyes on Jesus.*

Pray this prayer to Him:

O Lord Jesus, You know how cut off and lonely I've been feeling. Forgive me, Lord! I was acting like an atheist!

But now I come near to You, and according to Your promise in James 4:8, You have come near to me.

Lord, Psalm 16:8 says that in Your presence is fullness of joy! Then—

> "I delight to sit in [your] shade,
> and [your] fruit is sweet to my taste"
> (Song of Solomon 2:3).

Amen.

---

[2] See my book *Discipling One Another* (Waco: Word, Books, 1979).

Strong are the walls around me
That hold me all the day,
But they who thus have bound me
Cannot keep God away.
My very prison walls are dear
Because the God I love is here.

They know, who thus oppress me
'Tis hard to be alone,
But know not, One can bless me
Who comes through bars and stone:
He makes my dungeon's darkness bright
And fills my bosom with delight.

—Madame Jeanne Guyon (1648–1717),
      written when she was in solitary confinement,
      because of her Christian faith,
      in a prison in France

You who have no longer a mother to love you,
and yet crave for love,
God will be as a mother.
You who have no brother to help you,
and have so much need of support,
God will be your brother.
You who have no friends to comfort you,
and stand so much in need of consolation,
God will be your friend.

—*Gold Dust,*
a little centuries-old book
of unknown origin

6

Fix your eyes on Jesus
when others disappoint you

I told you before that I have a tendency to fuss. Any sin like that works seriously against you, because when you *do* have a legitimate complaint, people tend to shrug you off. Have you noticed?

Or sometimes I exaggerate. And then when I repeat statistics I know are right, my family tends to whittle down what I'm telling them. (Oh, don't you hate your sins? They always hurt us, laugh at us, reduce us!)

One Sunday morning I thought through a serious grievance I thought I had against Ray (honestly, I can't remember now what it was), and then I carefully laid it before him. He's normally thoughtful and kind, and I expected him to take me seriously. Ray's comment was, "Oh, Anne, you're fussing again," and he never heard my case at all.

My heart was still hurting later when we walked into church. Eventually the choir began to sing Mendelssohn's setting of Psalm 40:

> "I waited for the Lord;
>   He inclined unto me
>   [He leaned over and listened];
> He heard my complaint
>   [He took my grievance seriously!]."

At that moment I turned to *Him,* the One who could truly help. I fixed my eyes on *Him,* and I drew from Him sympathy and comfort and understanding of my legitimate distress.

(*"Oh, blessed,"* sang the choir, *"are they that hope and trust in Him."*)

I was blessed! My need was met, my heart was satisfied. Case closed.

Maybe you deal with such painful relationships, this story seems trivial. I've had far more painful ones, too, but the principle is the same: *Never expect any mere mortal to completely understand and support you.* No one ever could.

For that, *rush back to Jesus.* He is "the high priest who meets our need" (Hebrews 7:26).

And *rush to prayer:*

O Lord God, I've been leaning on a stick which can easily snap under my weight. And all the time You've been saying, "Come, lean on Me. I always listen to you, My child. I understand; I will hear and act."

Lord, when others disappoint me, I now receive this verse as my own: "We know and rely on the love God has for us" (1 John 4:16).

Lord, I want to love and respect and support my fellow humans; help me to do that. But I won't expect more from them than they can deliver.

Lord, I fix my eyes on You!
Amen.

What a sweet life is that [of fixing your eyes on Jesus]! The maintaining, strengthening it, has a softening influence; and it is a labor that never wearies, never deceives, but gives each day fresh cause for joy.

—*Gold Dust*

7

Fix your eyes on Jesus
when you're sad

If you're feeling sad, there's a reason. Perhaps you've recently experienced some kind of loss. Studies indicate that depression—sadness—and loss go together.

- *Have you ever lost your wallet?* The sudden feeling in the pit of your stomach is depression.
- *Have you lost someone dear to you?* Your mourning is a form of depression.
- *Did you recently lose your job, or have you been demoted?* Your loss of status will lead to depression.
- *Are you wondering if people around you are thinking less of you?* Even an *imaginary* loss of status will produce depression.
- *Ten years ago did your children make you proud, and now they embarrass you?* Your loss of relationship with them, as well as your very real loss of status as a parent, will bring depression.
- *Are you sick? Or are you worried that you might get sick?* A loss of health, or a possible projected loss of health, will bring depression.

- *Have you just finished a big project? Has there recently been a lot of excitement in your life?* A physical loss, even just a loss of adrenalin, will produce temporary depression until you get filled up again.

Maybe you can put your finger on why you're sad, maybe you can't. Either way, consider this:

If your depression, your sadness, is longer than brief, it starts to become your very dangerous enemy.

Many people don't realize what a threat sadness is—and any danger which is unrecognized as a danger is all the more dangerous. There is no stigma against sadness. There is no embarrassment, no alarm, no rushing to the Lord to eliminate it.

But God's Word says, "The joy of the Lord is your strength" (Nehemiah 8:10).

And when a Christian is sad—whether he realizes it or not, *his power is diminished and he's vulnerable.*

A country that has internal unrest is the least able to resist any threatening foreign power. And a believer with sadness inside is the least able to resist any attack of Satan.

Depression is a sinister "fifth column" at work within the Christian community.

You watch a rejected congregation after a church split: As long as they're sad, there will be little true worship, little evangelism; the people can't focus on anything but themselves.

You watch an individual Christian who's sad: He's necessarily self-centered. As long as he's sad he—or she—makes a poor marriage partner.

When we're sad, we're sick. We don't function well. We don't lift and encourage other believers, and we don't appeal to unbelievers. Our spiritual strength and effectiveness are cut down.

No wonder the great George Mueller used to say, "My first business every morning is to make sure that my soul is happy in Jesus!"

You're objecting. You're saying, "But, Anne, things happen in our lives. Sometimes you can't put on a Pollyanna grin and chirp 'Praise the Lord' and pretend everything is wonderful."

You're absolutely right.

There is a time for tears:

> over sin and its resulting human misery (Matthew 5:4),
> in the burden of ministering to others (Acts 20:31),
> in compassion over the plights of others (Nehemiah 1:4;
> Romans 12:15), and so on. . . .

In our living, we need to feel the full stretch of human emotions. When you need to cry—whether you're a man or a woman—let the tears flow and don't be ashamed.

When Lazarus died, *Jesus wept.*

Nevertheless, Jesus' very coming brought with it a great power to comfort and be comforted—a great new capacity for deep, overcoming joy!

He came . . .

> To comfort all that mourn . . .
> To give unto them beauty for ashes,
> the oil of joy for mourning,
> the garment of praise for the spirit of heaviness
> (Isaiah 61: 2–3, KJV).

He has taken away our susceptibility to a debilitating, long-term "spirit of heaviness."

"Do not let your hearts be troubled," He said (John 14:27). He wasn't saying, "There, there." He was saying, "Don't allow it! It's bad for you."

Paul in prison and facing death was God's mouthpiece for this command: "Rejoice in the Lord!" (Philippians 4:4).

It's not God's wish or His suggestion—it's His command. And it's for our best good. So He has Paul there in jail say it twice: "Rejoice in the Lord always. I will say it again: Rejoice!"

Personal joy is your strong defense against the world, the flesh, and the devil.

Maybe you're saying, "I really am sad these days. *What can I do to get joy back in my life?"*

Let me suggest a daily program for you to work on it.

(Above all, don't thrash around. Don't heave, don't pace, don't be overexcited. You can never free tangled thread by jerking and forcing it.)

1. Sit down before the Lord. Settle your mind in repose and calm.

2. Now think, "What are the knots in my tangledness—the specific situations in my life—that are giving me sadness?" Ask Him to put them in your mind; then write them in a list.

3. Now study slowly and carefully Philippians 4: 6–7:

Do not be anxious about anything, but in everything, by prayer and petition, with thanksgiving, present your requests to God [one knot—one item on your list—at a time].

And the peace of God, which transcends all understanding, will guard [shield] your hearts and minds in Christ Jesus.

4. In succession, work at each "knot" before the Lord, turning it this way and that, praying,"Lord, help. Lord, give me wisdom and solutions from You. I trust You. And by faith I examine this ugly knot *with thanksgiving."*

When you don't see a solution, let it go and turn to an easier knot. There are small ones God will help you free on the spot; tougher ones may depend on solving those first.

5. Now deliberately, in spite of your tangle, turn your full attention to Jesus; **fix your eyes on Him.**

Sing to Him; maybe sing a praise song. If all you know is "Jesus Loves Me," that's a great one. (Remember what music did for King Saul in 1 Samuel 16:23.)

As it says in Psalm 68: 3–4,

May the righteous be glad
    and rejoice before God;
        may they be happy and joyful.
Sing to God, sing praise to his name.

(Remember, "the righteous" aren't perfect people—in our eyes—they're the ones who have received Jesus as their Savior and so *God sees* them as righteous, or perfect! Wonderful! And He says His plan, His will, is for them to be happy and joyful.)

Whether you feel like it or not, make a program every day of these three:
1. In a spirit of relaxation, gently working those "knots" one at a time,
2. Bible reading,
3. Praise and singing.
"Let the afflicted . . . rejoice" (Psalm 34:2).

We got two letters in the mail today. One says,

> Our country is at war and our dear son is of prime drafting age, but we have peace in our hearts. Are we submitting to this? More than that, when God is in control we are actually *praising* Him for it.

The second letter is from a wife whose greatly loved husband has been found to have terminal cancer. She writes,

> God has given us the grace to face this, to speak and share it, and to believe that He is doing what is best. The last thing before surgery that Bill said to me was, "Remember no matter which way it goes it will be RIGHT!"

Of course behind the scenes there are tears, there is pain. . . . Moses went through every kind of turmoil, but "he persevered because he saw him who was invisible" (Hebrews 11:27).
Fix your eyes on Jesus and His solutions.

Maybe you're simply saying, "Anne, I just have too many knots. There's no hope; my life's a mess."
Let God speak to you, my dear friend, through His mouthpiece Habakkuk. He was facing international disasters on an overwhelming scale, and here's what he said:

Though the fig tree does not bud,
   and there are no grapes on the vines,
though the olive crop fails
   and the fields produce no food,
though there are no sheep in the pen
   and no cattle in the stalls. . .

[in other words, when everything all at once is absolutely terrible]

. . . yet I will rejoice in the Lord,
I will be joyful in God my Savior.
The Sovereign Lord is my strength;
he makes my feet like the feet of a deer,
he enables me to go on the heights" (Habakkuk 3:17–19).

God wants you "on the heights"—to live above it all—in Him, with Him.
"Above the clouds the sun is always shining."

Let's talk to the Lord about your sadness:

Thank You, Lord God, for alerting me to this danger. "Restore to me the joy of your salvation" (Psalm 51:12).

I don't see solutions yet, but I see that my sadness is the first part of the problem.

Lord, relax me. Help me right now to **fix my eyes on Jesus**.

And then, Lord, discipline me—to begin this daily program before You to overcome my sadness.

"I rejoice in following your statutes as one rejoices in great riches" (Psalm 119:14).

In Christ's name of power and authority, amen.

*. . . Then a new set of eyes
(so to speak) will develop within us,
enabling us to be looking at Jesus
while our outward eyes are seeing
the scenes of this passing world. . . .*
—A.W. Tozer

8

Fix your eyes on Jesus
when you're dissatisfied

I remember a period in our life when Ray and I felt God had put us on too tight a leash. Have you ever felt that way, or do you now? We felt restricted, confined. We wanted breathing room. We were singing, "Don't fence me in!"

It was a very important time for us. God wanted to teach us Psalm 131:

> My heart is not proud, O Lord,
>> my eyes are not haughty;
> I do not concern myself with great matters
>> or things too wonderful for me.
> But I have stilled and quieted my soul;
>> like a weaned child with its mother,
>> like a weaned child is my soul within me.
> O Israel, put your hope in the Lord
>> both now and forevermore.

Do you think anything concerning you right now is too small?
   Your house or apartment?
   Your personal reputation?
   Your influence?
   Your job?
   Your family (you want to add a spouse or children)?
   Your circle of friends?
   Your salary?
   Your *life?*

Until I paid attention to Psalm 131, I chafed. Then I discovered that God's leash wasn't too tight; my heart was too proud! I thought I "deserved" more; my self-image had greater expectations. And that attitude was the very grease on which I slid into self-pity, discontent, ungratefulness, misery.

Then *I fixed my eyes on Jesus*—and in my own eyes I became smaller and smaller. What was my stature, my purity, my power, my excellence compared with His?

I felt foolish, embarrassed, very small.

And now what did I deserve? Nothing—nothing at all. I was an "unworthy servant" (Luke 17:10).

Now I looked at all that the Lord God in His incredible grace had lavished on me—with such love and joy—and it was like Christmas in July!

Notice what God can do for small people:
When Gideon told the Lord that he was small—"My clan is the weakest in Manasseh, and I am the least in my family" (Judges 6:15)—*then God could give him a big place:* He made him leader of His people.

When Saul said to God that he was small—"Am I not a Benjamite, from the smallest tribe in Israel, and is my clan not the least of all the clans of the tribe of Benjamin?" (1 Samuel 9:21)—*then God could give him a huge place:* He anointed him king over all Israel.

(Later God reminded him why He could elevate him: because "you were . . . small in your own eyes," 1 Samuel 15:17. When he turned proud, the Lord demoted him again.)

When you're dissatisfied, where are your eyes?
Mine were on myself, and the result was sheer misery.

Discontent drives you to want more and more, to expect more and more, and to develop a spirit of disappointment both with your own life and with God—which is death to your soul.

> Lust in final form spends
> everything
> To purchase headstones.
> All passions die in
> graveyards.[1]

Fix your eyes again on your blessed Jesus. He is full of grace and goodness; trust Him. *Be satisfied. Be thankful.*

> I have stilled and quieted my soul
> like a weaned child. . . .

God had to help me grow out of babyhood and get a right perspective on myself. A baby thinks he's the center of the universe, so he fusses and cries.

Look at Jesus and all that He is. Shrink until you fit your space. Now compare yourself with so many others around the world who are in a smaller place than you. Shrink some more.

> Humble yourselves . . . under God's mighty hand, that he
> may lift you up in due time (1 Peter 5:6).

---

[1] "A Symphony in Sand," quoted in *Christianity Today* Magazine, 24 September 1990, "Reflections," p. 41.

Fix your eyes on Jesus, and He will continually "set [your] feet in a spacious place" (Psalm 31:8).

Now why don't you pray to Him:

Lord, forgive my restlessness, my dissatisfaction. I acknowledge my ingratitude. Lord, I rest in You! And I consecrate myself to develop the habit of thankfulness and contentment.

"I have stilled and quieted my soul." I worship You! You are nothing but good, and You give me all the good things that are now good for me.

Alleluia! Amen.

O my Savior,
    help me.
I am so slow to learn, so prone to forget, so weak to climb;
I am in the foothills when I should be on the heights;
I am pained by my graceless heart,
    my prayerless days,
    my poverty of love,
    my sloth in the heavenly race,
    my sullied conscience,
    my wasted hours,
    my unspent opportunities.
I am blind while light shines around me:
    take the scales from my eyes. . . .
Make it my chief joy to study thee,
    meditate on thee,
    gaze on thee,
    sit like Mary at thy feet,
    lean like John on thy breast,
    appeal like Peter to thy love,
    count like Paul all things dung. . . .
Let not faith cease from seeking thee
until it vanishes into sight.
Ride forth in me, thou king of kings and lord of lords,
    that I may live victoriously, and in victory attain my
    end.

—Old Puritan prayer

9

Fix your eyes on Jesus
when you're angry

I have a memory of anger which is so childish I should have forgotten it—but I haven't. I can't.

I was a little girl, and my mother and I were having a tea party with my doll dishes. She was a great mom! But she said something that made me so frustrated I hit her arm, and the tea spilled all over everything. Some kind of timing—I ruined the whole party. I still feel bad when I think of it.

No matter the age, "A fool gives full vent to his anger" (Proverbs 29:11).

If you are angry at someone right now, you know the feeling in the pit of your stomach, and you know the words that race through your mind—words to tell that person and then words to tell others so they'll get on your side. . . .

Wait!

Wait. Cool down. Be quiet a minute. Think.

Look at Jesus. He "endured" (Hebrews 12:2). He had every reason to be legitimately angry: Stupid, terrible people had unjustly done Him in—and yet He said,

> Father, forgive them, for they do not know what they are doing (Luke 23:34).

You need some kind of spiritual disciplines to change your mental habit pattern. Perhaps even this little visual aid will do.

Get two sets of paper, one for your mornings and one for your evenings. Post them around in all the strategic spots where you can check your attitude.

On some of the papers write this:

"HIS COMPASSIONS NEVER FAIL.
THEY ARE NEW EVERY MORNING."
(LAMENTATIONS 3:22–23)

Post them where you'll see them as you start each day: on the bathroom mirror, by the coffee pot. When you see them, commit your heart to feel compassion all that day for that person at whom you've been angry.

On other pieces of paper write this:

"DO NOT LET THE SUN GO DOWN
WHILE YOU ARE STILL ANGRY."
(EPHESIANS 4:26)

Post them where you'll see them as your day starts to wind down: on your car dashboard as you drive home from work, in your kitchen as you start to fix the evening meal.

Then on a special paper check off each morning and each sundown that God has helped you overcome your anger. And continue this for however long it takes to *melt that anger out of your heart and make you forgiving and compassionate and tender.*

You see, *the problem isn't really the person who's troubling you; it's within you.* All your life, sinners around you will sin—it's what they do best!

But fix your eyes on Jesus. Remember His words:

> Love is patient, love is kind. . . . It is not easily angered, it keeps no record of wrongs. . . . It always protects, always trusts, always hopes, always perseveres. Love never fails (1 Corinthians 13:4–8).

If anger is your problem, you may suddenly realize that *Jesus' eye is fixed on you,* studying you, and He asks you simply, "Doest thou well to be angry?" (John 4:9, KJV. In other words, "Is this improving you?")

Man's anger does not bring about the righteous life that God desires (James 1:20).

Then pray this prayer to Him:

Lord, I refuse to fix my eyes on my "troubler"; then I get upset and feel abused and cheated and angry. *I fix my eyes on You.* Then my heart will melt, and I'll become like You—kind, compassionate, loving, forgiving. Help me, Lord!

In Your own dear name, amen.

Don't forget to post those pieces of paper!

Equipment can break down or get lost,
  water can leak away,
    records can be destroyed by fire,
  the minister can be delayed
    or the church burn down.
All these are external and subject to accident
  or mechanical failure. . . .
But looking is of the heart,
  and can be done successfully by anybody—
    standing up
    or kneeling down
    or lying in [your] last agony,
      a thousand miles from any church.

—A.W. Tozer, *The Pursuit of God* (pp. 94, 95)

10

Fix your eyes on Jesus
when you're tempted

Temptation. A new one comes every day of the week.

Tomorrow is Sunday morning, and I'm here in the house all alone for the weekend—for long, precious hours to work on this book. The deadline is near.

Ray is at the National Religious Broadcasters' convention in Washington. He won't know if I go to church or not.

Melinda, our secretary, would normally be there, but she and John are out of town for the weekend. She wouldn't know.

The children are all involved in ministries in their own churches. They wouldn't know.

The church has two morning services; each of my friends would think I'd gone to the other one.

And here's the real cruncher: I just got the worst haircut of my entire life.

Lord, this once, couldn't I just stay holed up at home and keep writing about everybody's fixing their eyes on You?

Temptation!

Words from my own book *Up with Worship* come back to haunt me:

> Worship is fundamentally an offering. . . .
>
> Back in Old Testament days it was clear to see that worship involved giving. You came to the tabernacle or temple with your offering in your hand, or in your arms!— lugging it, or dragging it, maybe. It might have been wheat or oil, but often it was a sheep or goat or young bull. . . .
>
> And this is what worship still means today. Hebrews 13:15 says, "Through Jesus, therefore, let us continually offer to God a sacrifice of praise. . . ."
>
> The praise is to be continuous—which sometimes means inconvenient. It will take effort. . . .
>
> Sometimes you may be critically busy—when every minute of the day is precious, to get something done. Well, drag that lamb of two hours' time, and come to God's house. . . . Bring to Him your consistent, sacrificial gift of worship.
>
> Drag that lamb![1]

I hate it when my own words order me around. (Once Ray was driving on the freeway, feeling depressed. He turned on the radio and his own voice said, "CHEER UP!" Ray scoffed, "Yeah, yeah, but what do *you* know about it?")

I'm going to church, of course. Would a cover-everything hat help? Well, I mustn't fix my eyes on myself. . . .

Late Sunday morning. Between my last words and now, I was hit with another, far more insidious temptation.

Last night I got into bed putting together in my head a story for this book which was almost true, but ever-so-slightly embellished—I could see in my mind's eye it would look just right on paper.

And there on television was an exposé of an itinerant preacher/healer who for years has "preached the Word" and cried "Praise Jesus" with the best of them. He's done it all. But

---

[1] *Up with Worship*, pp. 47–48.

now he's finally confessing that he's never even had a leaning toward the Christian religion! So after years of fraud, he's finally getting out of "the business."

Saddened and shocked, I vowed to straighten out my story, and I recommitted myself to honesty before the Lord in every part of me.

This morning the choir sang "Panis Angelicus":

> And in temptation's hour,
> Save through Thy mighty power. . . .

And during the quiet of the prelude, my eyes had fallen on Psalm 119: 29–30:

> Keep me from deceitful ways . . .
> I have chosen the way of truth.

The sacrificial animals of Leviticus 1:9 *were washed in their inner parts*, to be "pleasing to the Lord."

> How much more, then, will the blood of Christ . . .
> cleanse our consciences . . . so that we may serve the living
> God! (Hebrews 9:14)

Are you tempted right now, and your mind is coaxing you to yield?

Or your emotions are strongly pulling you to yield?

Or your body is screaming at you to yield?

Quick—*force those eyes of yours to be fixed on Jesus.* He was tempted, too, you know.

And *notice three things:*

1. *God didn't cause Jesus' temptations, but He did allow them.* "Jesus was led by the Spirit into the desert to be tempted by the devil" (Matthew 4:1).

2. *His temptations were truly painful.* "He . . . suffered when he was tempted" (Hebrews 2:18).

3. But He never once yielded. "We have [a High Priest] who has been tempted in every way, just as we are—yet was without sin" (Hebrews 4:15).

And look at the same three things about your own temptations:
1. God doesn't cause them, but He does allow them. "When tempted, no one should say, 'God is tempting me' . . . Each one is tempted when, by his own evil desire, he is dragged away and enticed" (James 1:13–14).

Be careful about that old saw, "You can't keep the birds from landing on your head—just don't let them build a nest in your hair." We use it to say, "It's no big deal if I'm tempted. Jesus was tempted, too."

Listen, you're not Jesus! *Flap your arms!* When they see your head or mine, they're positively *tempted* to land on us! These proverbial buzzards see inside of us our "evil desire," as James says, and they chirp, "Come on, everybody, that sucker's an easy touch. We can settle in there for sure." Then, as James goes on to say, the evil desire leads to sin, and the sin leads to death!

And it all began with what we thought was a harmless little temptation.

2. Your temptations, like Jesus,' are truly painful.
Run from them! Avoid them! Don't hang out where they might be! Jesus says, "Watch and pray so that you will not fall into temptation" (Matthew 26:41).

Over four hundred years ago Francis de Sales wrote,

As soon as you perceive yourself tempted, follow the example of children when they see a wolf or a bear in the country, for they immediately run into the arms of their father or mother. . . .

Run in spirit to embrace the holy cross, as if you saw our Savior Jesus Christ crucified before you. Protest that you never will consent to the temptation, implore his assistance against it, and still refuse your consent as long as the temptation shall continue.

But . . . *look not the temptation in the face, but look only to our Lord* (italics mine).[2]

Why? Because every time you fix your eyes on the temptation, you'll be that much weaker and more apt to yield.

"When the woman **saw** . . . the fruit of the tree . . . she **took** . . . it" (Genesis 3:6).

"Achan . . . **saw** . . . the plunder . . . and . . . **took** them" (Joshua 7:20–21).

"David . . . **saw** a woman . . . and **took** her" (2 Samuel 11:2, KJV).

Watch, for instance, what you absorb of the daily news. Dirty people love dirt; that's why so much of the news is about dirt. So you, too, take it into your mind, you picture it, you imagine it. . . . Now your own mind is dirty as well. And from a dirty mind spring dirty acts. The news media are powerful transmitters of moral diseases.

If you're struggling with such a big temptation that you're frightened, rush to a godly older person for counsel. Even the humiliation of confessing the temptation will strengthen you against it.

But it's not usually the big temptations that undo us, it's the lesser ones. It's not usually the wolves and bears that defeat us, it's the flies!

Which is harder for you to resist, murder or anger?

Adultery or those exciting but treacherous little flirtations?

Stealing or coveting?

Vile actions or vile thoughts?

Mafia connections or craftiness and scheming?

Oh, the flies, the flies! Eventually they can make you feel as corrupted as if you were a chronic liar or a drunk.

This is all-out war. As long as you live, don't let down your guard.

But here's the good news:

3. *You don't have to yield.* "God is faithful; he will not let you be tempted beyond what you can bear. But when you

2. Frances de Sales, *Introduction to a Devout Life*, pp. 298–299.

are tempted, he will also provide a way out so that you can stand up under it" (1 Corinthians 10:13).

"Because [Jesus] himself suffered when he was tempted, he is able to help those who are being tempted" (Hebrews 2:18).

So what do you do when you're tempted? **You fix your eyes not on the temptation, but on Jesus.** Then you'll "find grace to help . . . in [your] time of need" (Hebrews 4:16).

Dear Herman Wobbema! He knew that grace. Herman was a beautiful older man in our Lake Avenue Church, almost stone deaf, with a million-dollar smile.

Once in the middle of an evening service Ray suddenly held a microphone right to Herman's mouth; he was sitting in an aisle seat. Unforewarned, Herman said gently into the mike,

> "Through many dangers, toils and snares
> I have already come.
> 'Tis grace hath brought me safe thus far,
> And grace will lead me home."

He never heard what followed: the whole congregation's spontaneous applause.

Why don't you pray,

O Father, I'd like to end my life like that! You know my dangers, my toils, my snares—but You promised they'll never be more than I can bear.

O Jesus, for courage and victory I call on Your grace. **I fix my eyes on You.** Amen.

11

Fix your eyes on Jesus when world conditions make you afraid

Ray tells me that once when he was a little boy playing in the park, he forgot that a seesaw isn't a slide. He slid down the board of the seesaw and painfully lodged a huge splinter in his bottom. It was too much for his big sisters to take out, so they escorted him to Dr. Lincoln's house, which was near the park.

Dr. Lincoln was their gruff, kindly, beetlebrowed old family physician, and he knew them all well. So when he looked at little Ray, the youngest of the five Ortlund children, who was teary-eyed and somewhat in shock, Dr. Lincoln knew just what he had to do.

First, with his arm tight around Ray, he explained he was going to have to cut that thing out, and it would hurt like all blazes. But Dr. Lincoln said he'd be right there to do a good job and then pour in plenty of iodine to keep out the bugs and make it heal well. Then, he said, just give it some time and Ray would be good as new.

After this thorough and realistic explanation, there was one final word on what you did to get through the hurt: you yelled "Hold 'em, East High!" just as loud as you could.

Now, this was East Des Moines, Iowa, and every little kid in East Des Moines grew up idolizing the football players at East High. Those guys were totally rough and tough.

Then old Dr. Lincoln put Ray across his lap and went to work on his naked little rear. And the only anesthetic was both of them bellowing at the top of their lungs, "Hold 'em, East High! Hold 'em, East High!"

That's a very homey illustration . . . but *the Lord Jesus Christ knew when He was here the first time that we'd all have experiences before He came back that would hurt like all blazes.*

So in Luke 21 He gave us a realistic description of how bad our world was going to get, so we'd be prepared. He said He wanted us to know what to expect:

> Watch out that you are not deceived (v. 8).

And then He painted a black picture:

> Nation will rise against nation, and kingdom against kingdom, and there will be earthquakes and famines in many lands, and epidemics, and terrifying things happening in the heavens (vv. 10–11, TLB).

He spoke particularly of how believers would be hassled and dragged off to prison and some even put to death. And—

> When you see Jerusalem surrounded by armies, you will know that its desolation is near (v. 20).

Now, in a sense, like old Dr. Lincoln, Jesus was describing all this with one arm around us, soothing us. He said,

> Do not be frightened (v. 9).

That's a command!
And He said,

> Make up your mind not to worry (v. 14).

It's a deliberate act of your will.

When world conditions are terrible and enemies threaten, remember Genesis 12:6–7:

> The Canaanites were then in the land, *but the Lord appeared to Abram* (italics mine).

When the enemy seems close, *Jesus is closer.* And He commands you to "fear not" 365 times in the Bible—once for each new day.

> Then *don't fix your eyes on what's making you afraid.*
> And *don't fix your eyes on your fear.*
> When you're afraid, *fix your eyes on Jesus.*

Best of all, He said to us,

> When these things begin to come to pass, then *look up, and lift up your heads;* for your redemption draweth near (Luke 21:28, KJV, italics mine).

When you hear newscasts and discussions and all the daily street talk, when people are begin to "faint from terror, apprehensive of what is coming on the world" (v. 26), *fix your eyes on Jesus.*

> Do not fear what they fear,
> and do not dread it (Isaiah 8:12).

Before long, all this will be over.

See [He says], I am coming soon, and my reward is with
me (Revelation 22:12).

"Hold 'em, East High!"

Pray to Him about this:

O Lord Jesus, give me great compassion for this hurting
world; may I testify of You and bring Your wonderful salvation and help wherever I can.

But, Lord, meanwhile, keep me obediently looking up
and not being afraid. *May my eyes be fixed on You and Your
glorious return to set things right at last!*

Maranatha! "Even so, come, Lord Jesus" (Revelation
22:20)! Amen.

I heard the voice of Jesus say,
      "I am this dark world's light;
      Look unto Me, thy morn shall rise,
      And all thy day be bright."
I looked to Jesus, and I found
In Him my Star, my Sun;
And in that Light of life I'll walk
Till traveling days are done.

—Horatius Bonar, 1846

12

Fix your eyes on Jesus when you're misunderstood or mistreated

If you are now suffering at the hands of others,

Or if you have in the past and you're still suffering over those memories—

Is there anything harder to bear than undeserved suffering? Well, fix your eyes on Jesus. It sounds like a cliché but it's not, by any means. What does Jesus have to say to you?

The Lord Jesus knew that suffering is part of God's perfect and loving will. Ouch, that doesn't sound like good news! Keep reading; it's going to be.

> This suffering is all part of the work God has given
> you. Christ, who suffered for you, is your example . . .
> (1 Peter 2:21, TLB).

Christians who don't believe their suffering is "of the Lord" turn out weak and unstable. At any encounters with pain they're apt to cry for immediate deliverance, thinking it's of the devil, or else they turn and run—from a job, a church, a marriage, whatever the cause of the pain.

Maybe they've never noticed Philippians 1:29—

> For to you has been given the privilege not only of trusting him but also of suffering for him (TLB).

Trusting and suffering: the two come as a package. You take one, you get the other with it.

You take salvation from a good Father, you get the privilege of suffering from the same good Father.

You say "thank you" for one, you say "thank you" for the other (1 Thessalonians 5:18).

Understanding this simple truth makes strong, sturdy, un-flappable believers. Through the worst circumstances their heads are up. Said Job, "Shall we accept good from God, and not trouble?"

Listen: your suffering isn't—or wasn't—really given to you by bad or thoughtless people. (If it were, you could hate them or want to get even.)

No, *it's God Himself, your wonderful Father, who*—through people or circumstances—*puts suffering into your life. He lovingly allows it.*

> The testing of your faith develops perseverance. Persever-ance must finish its work so that you may be mature and complete, not lacking anything (James 1:3–4).

He's shaping you by those pressures, so you will turn out wonderful. He's perfecting you.

> He knows the way that [you] take; when he has tested [you, you will] come forth as gold (Job 23:10).

I'm counting on that. Ray and I spent some miserable years in a church where we didn't fit. It wasn't their fault! They're wonderful people and we still love them dearly; but we were just going different directions. The pain was terrible. But how valuable that suffering was for us! Ministering as we constantly do to pastors and spouses, we would have been too glib, too self-assured, too full of easy answers, too unsympathetic—without that crashing failure in our own career.

And you, too, like the Lord Jesus Himself, are "made perfect through suffering" (Hebrews 2:10).

He was oppressed and afflicted . . .
Yet it was the Lord's will to crush him and cause him to suffer (Isaiah 53:7, 10).

So what did Jesus do, to give you clues for what to do in your situation?

Hebrews 12:2 says to fix your eyes on Jesus because:
1. "For the joy set before him [he] endured the cross."
And if you, too, "hang in there," your personal glory will follow as well:

Our present sufferings are not worth comparing with the glory that will be revealed in us (Romans 8:18).

It won't be long! Jesus didn't run; He "endured." You do the same.

2. *But he scorned its shame.* Think about this carefully.
To "scorn" means to "belittle." Jesus didn't scorn the *cross*— to suffer on the cross for the sins of the world was a Big Deal. And for you to be called by God to participate in His sufferings (1 Peter 4:13)—that's a Big Deal, too. Appreciate it.
But the *shame* of the cross He did scorn; He took that part of it lightly. He thought little of His own humiliation, His own feelings. He wasn't self-centered, self-pitying.

3. *Even in the midst of His suffering, He was still concerned for others.* "Dear woman, here is your son . . . Here is your mother" (John 19: 26–27).

4. He had true compassion for those who hurt Him. "Father, forgive them" (Luke 23:34). No bitterness, no vengeful thoughts, no demanding of rights.

5. "He entrusted himself to him who judges justly" (1 Peter 2:23).He prayed, "Father, into your hands I commit my spirit" (Luke 23:46).

If you feel totally misunderstood—or if you have in the past,
If you suffer at the hands of others—or if in the past you did,
Right now, as you're reading this, *pray this prayer:*

Lord, for my own maturing, to make me more like Christ, You've allowed me to participate in His sufferings. I'm awed. I'm honored to be in such company. That's a Big Deal.
But, Lord, I choose to belittle my own feelings. They're not a big deal. Keep me from retaliation, real or imagined; keep me from filling my thoughts with self-pity and fresh self-woundings and all over-occupation with myself.
Lord, keep my heart and life concerned for others.
Lord, give me true compassion for my oppressors.
And, Lord, I entrust myself totally to You. Into Your good hands I commit my spirit. Amen.

You're released! You're free! Your heart has begun a deep process of healing! Hold your head high!
Fixing your eyes on Jesus has lifted you above all your oppression. God is using it as an instrument to perfect you,
mature you,
make you whole.
"Consider it pure joy" (James 1:2).

Now you can read Romans 12:14–21 with new clarity:

Bless those who persecute you. . . .

Do not repay anyone evil for evil. . . . Do not take revenge . . . but leave room for God's wrath, for it is written: "It is mine to avenge; I will repay," says the Lord. On the contrary:

"If your enemy is hungry, feed him; if he is thirsty, give him something to drink. . . ."

Do not be overcome by evil, but overcome evil with good.

O Lord Jesus, I, Anne Ortlund, take this for myself as well. Help me not to write one thing and act another. May writer pray for reader, and reader for writer, that when we are misunderstood or mistreated, we may fix our eyes on You. Amen.

13

Fix your eyes on Jesus
when you struggle financially

Our family has lived for several months at a time here and there overseas. Before we went the first time, we thought that *Americans are worldly and materialistic because they have so much.*

Then we discovered that *Christians overseas can be worldly and materialistic even though they have little.* Their focus can be on what they *don't* have—talking constantly about their high taxes, their low wages, how wonderful America must be, their frustrations over lacking this and lacking that. . . .

Then we began thinking about Christians we know, American or otherwise, who are wealthy but not worldly, material-rich but not materialistic. They're responsible or even lavish in their giving: *Their eyes are on Jesus.*

And we know "poor" Christians who are the same!

And we thought, *being materialistic means being too aware of the material, whether you have much or little.*

For years Ray and I knew a famous California orange rancher—he's in heaven now—who gave to the Lord of his time and money beyond all human reasoning. Elbow-deep in ministry, he had little time to oversee his ranches. Privately one time he said to me as he shook his head in wonder, "Anne, it seems as if the more I stay away from those oranges, the more the Lord makes them multiply!" This man's eyes were truly fixed on Jesus.

Then Ray and I have a dear friend who spent most of her adult life as a nanny in a wealthy home, and when she reached retirement age ten years ago, they turned her out without a cent. I know very few of the miracle-stories about how God pays her apartment rent and keeps her from month to month, although I know her well. She's always too busy talking about other things: the schoolchildren's choir she helps with, the balloons she's blown up for somebody's birthday party, the fun she's having caring for some shut-in. . . . Her eyes are continually on Jesus, and He Himself provides for her.

Does this all sound too glib?

Do I sound insensitive to your struggles?

God has given Ray and me struggles, too. He gave us early-marriage poverty, with three babies and simply not enough food money to last between those small paychecks. He gave us later poverty, when at the age most people retire we got stripped of our life savings. And along the way He gave us sudden joblessness, not of our choosing. . . .

Look, Jesus Himself lived His earthly life in both poverty and serenity. He had almost nothing, and yet—for instance—He was confident that His Father would provide an upper room for the Last Supper. . . .

Our friend Jim says, "Boy, it was so freeing when I discovered that my income isn't my source of supply, God is! God knows my needs; my income doesn't know my needs! So I don't depend on my income, I depend on Him."

The eyes of all look to you,
    and you give them their food at the proper time.
You open your hand
    and satisfy the desires of every living thing (Psalm 145:15–16).

To be dependent on your own supplies is bondage. To be dependent on Him (the One who promises over and over to supply your need)—*this is freedom.*

But let me ask you a question:
    Is your cash shortage temporary or chronic?
If it's temporary, wait upon Him for supply.
If you're chronically cash-short, something is wrong, because that doesn't fit with all His promises. Think about them:

The Lord is my shepherd;
    I shall not want (Psalm 23:1).

He provides food for those who fear him;
    he remembers his covenant forever (Psalm 111:5).

The Lord does not let the righteous go hungry (Proverbs 10:3).

So *what's the problem,* here? Search for it. Go to a financial advisor—best of all, a godly older couple or person you know who seems to have been wise in handling money.

Maybe you're overspending; you want too much too soon. The Lord says that's sin (Luke 15:13–18). Ask for help to set up a budget, and ask your advisor to hold you accountable to stick to it.

Maybe you're under-giving; the Lord says that's sin, too (Haggai 1:5–9). At the top of your budget items put your tithe (ten percent of your income), and make that the first check you write with every incoming paycheck.

Correct what you see isn't right—and then trust Him, trust Him, trust Him!

You can't support yourself any more than you could create yourself. Leave to God the things that only God can do.

So don't fix your eyes on your bills, your problems, your needs—He "knows that you need them" (Matthew 6:32).

Fix your eyes on Jesus.

Let's pray to Him.

Abba Father, Your Word is so full of Your wonderful promises to care for me. Then help me to relax in my heart, to live by faith and not by sight.

O Lord, give me wisdom for earning, spending, saving, and giving. And then help me to *fix my eyes on You* for supply.

I thank You for seasons of plenty, and I thank You for seasons of want—both (Philippians 4:12, 13). Both are from Your loving hand, according to my deepest need.

I trust You! In Christ's strong name, amen.

"All things are yours;
All are yours,
and you are of Christ,
and Christ is of God"
(1 Corinthians 3:21–23).

When you see that Christ is everything,
and you make Him your everything,
then you have everything.

14

Fix your eyes on Jesus
when you've struck it rich

Do you have lots of money, at least comparably speaking?

Can you buy nice clothes, live in a nice house, do things some others can't do?

It's important for you to see that importance isn't very important.

Here's something Francis de Sales said in 1609 (and I don't understand 1609 humor, so I don't know if he was being funny or serious, but he makes his point):

> Some [people] become proud and insolent, either by riding a good horse, wearing a feather in their hat, or by being dressed in a fine suit of clothes; but who does not see the folly of this?
>
> For if there be any glory in such things, the glory belongs to the horse, the bird, and the tailor;
>
> And what meanness of heart must it be, to borrow esteem from a horse. . . .

Or again, he's teaching a strong lesson but he expresses it with his own funny little quirk:

Certainly nothing can so effectively humble us before the mercy of God as the multitude of His benefits!

Whatever there is of good in us is not from ourselves. Do mules cease to be disgusting beasts, because they are laden with the precious and perfumed goods of the prince?

Well, so much for our self-esteem.
The Lord Himself says it best:

Who makes you different from anyone else? What do you have that you did not receive? And if you did receive it, why do you boast as though you did not? (1 Corinthians 4:7).

If you yourself have worked hard to make your money, listen to Him:

You may say to yourself, "My power and the strength of my hands have produced this wealth for me." But remember the Lord your God, for it is he who gives you the ability to produce wealth (Deuteronomy 8:17–18).

The immensely rich and successful King David, after publicly offering to God literally tons of gold and silver from his own personal treasuries, prayed in front of all his subjects,

Yours, O Lord, is the greatness and the power and the glory and the majesty and the splendor, for everything in heaven and earth is yours. . . .

Wealth and honor come from you. . . .

Everything comes from you, and we have given you only what comes from your hand (1 Chronicles 29:11–14).

God is in charge of all distributions of moneys and goods. And He's pleased and delighted to give them in abundance to someone like David who acknowledges Him as the source and who is diligent to give back responsibly and generously.

Centuries-old *Gold Dust,* that classic little book, says it this way:

> Do not hesitate to ask for temporal blessings—health, intellect, success. [God] can bestow them, and [He] never fails to do so where they tend to make the soul more holy.

Ah, there! That's the point! Will more riches make you more holy? Then God is perfectly willing to give them to you.

Now, read carefully, because this could make all the difference in your life: *People of this world work only for the love of themselves. You must work for the love of God.*

You see, self-love is full of jealousy, greed, uneasiness, and turbulence, and all the care and maintenance of that self-love is the same. Is that the kind of life you want, the kind of person you want to be?

But the love of God is sweet, productive, fulfilling, and agreeable. And the care and maintenance of your love for God— even working in the meantime for worldly goods—will be the same!

Would you like that kind of life? Would you like to be that kind of person?

Hold out your hands and cup them, and in your imagination fill them with all your money and possessions.

(Maybe you and your spouse would like to do this together, and put in your hands your wallets and checkbooks and some C.D. certificates or whatever, as symbolic of all the rest.)

Then read out loud David's prayer in 1 Chronicles 29:10– 13, and worship the Lord for all His goodness to you. If you'd like to make it a time of special giving to the Lord—a thank offering—you could continue praying verses 14 through 18.

Oh, my friend, in your strategic and responsible and happy circumstance of having money—

Fix your eyes on Jesus.

Once it was the blessing,
*   Now it is the Lord;*
Once it was the feeling,
*   Now it is His Word;*
Once His gifts I wanted,
*   Now the Giver own;*
Once I sought for healing,
*   Now Himself alone.*

—A. B. Simpson

PART 2

Fix your eyes on Jesus
to reshape your life

15

Fix your eyes on Jesus
for setting your goals

I have the ugliest, most comfy, most loved pair of old sweats. And I have the ugliest, most comfy, most loved pair of old Nikes. I tell Melinda, our secretary, I'm gonna wear my sweats and Nikes in heaven forever—unless I'm not supposed to wear anything at all. In which case, by then I'll look terrific.

Normally I only wear those uglies when I run, which is in our own neighborhood and pretty private. But the other day I had them on when I ducked briefly into the office, and Melinda and Ray both hooted when they saw my backside. I had a big split in the seam where I sit down.

This called for drastic action. I absolutely hate to sew, but that night I sat down with needle and thread and laboriously put my dear old sweats back together again.

Which is to say, no matter the awkwardness or pain or inconvenience, *most of us manage to do what we most want to do.*

What do you most want to do in your life? Whether you're following a carefully written list of personal goals or playing it by ear, *you're probably doing it.*

What is it you somehow manage to make room for, no matter what else must be sacrificed?

> Feeling good?
> Reading?
> Television?
> Weekends away in the R.V.?
> Your wardrobe?
> Your house?
> Certain relationships?
> Your job or career?
> Bowling?
> Skiing?
> Keeping up on the news?

Don't excuse, don't deceive yourself. *Scrutinize your life to see if you have loves unworthy of eternity that are sacrosanct, inviolable.* If you do, they're the "weights" of Hebrews 12:1. In themselves they're not sins, but they will certainly hinder you.

And they degrade you: They make sure you don't get to be that great man or woman of God that you could otherwise become.

What a waste.

What a tragedy.

Listen to the final paragraph of Ray's little book, *Lord, Make My Life a Miracle*:

> Your danger and mine is not that we become criminals, but rather that we become respectable, decent, commonplace, mediocre Christians. The twentieth-century temptations that really sap our spiritual power are the television, banana cream pie, the easy chair, and the credit card. *The Christian wins or loses in those seemingly innocent little moments of decision.*
>
> Lord, make my life a miracle![1]

-----

[1] p. 151.

Right now, fix your eyes on Jesus.

How can you get ready for that moment in eternity when you stand before Him?

> For we must all appear before the judgment seat of Christ, that each one may receive what is due him, for the things done while in the body, whether good or bad (2 Corinthians 5:10).

Verse 9 of that same passage answers how you get ready:

> So we make it our goal to please him.

Above all else—*your goal to please Him!* You scratch and claw for this; for this you discipline yourself; you get others to hold you accountable.

Come hell or high water, *you stretch to be, to do, what pleases Him.* Whatever it costs you, it's worth it. It's the fine pearl which you sell everything you've got to buy (Matthew 13: 45–46).

To please Him you sacrifice, if need be,

> feeling good,
> reading,
> television,
> weekends away in the R.V.,
> your wardrobe,
> your house,
> certain relationships,
> your job or career,
> your bowling,
> your skiing,
> your keeping up on the news . . . .

It's your life goal: to please Him.

And it will break down into more specific yearly goals, maybe three-month goals, today's goals. Make them practical; make them measurable.

Pleasing Him will work out differently in your life than in anyone else's, because He has made you unique.

For [you] are God's workmanship, created in Christ Jesus
to do good works, which God prepared in advance for [only
you] to do (Ephesians 2:10).

Be very careful, then, how you live; understand what
the Lord's will is (5:15, 17).

*"And get tough," says 1 Corinthians 9: "Don't pamper your
body; beat it and make it your slave!"*

"Do you not know that in a race all the runners run, but
only one gets the prize? Run in such a way as to get the
prize. Everyone who competes in the games goes into strict
training" (1 Corinthians 9: 24–25).

Let's pray.

O Lord, I deliberately refuse to gaze fondly at my toys, my
conveniences, my pleasures, my comfort zones. I want to
fix my eyes on You. I want to make it my life goal, and my
day-by-day goal, to please You.

As the eyes of slaves look to the hand of their master,
As the eyes of a maid look to the hand of her mistress,
So [my] eyes look to [you] (Psalm 123:2).

Show me Your will, O Lord, and help me to do it. That's
what *You* most want, and now that's what *I* most want—so
it will please us both. For Your own sake, amen.

I thank thee for showing me the vast difference
between knowing things by reason
and knowing them by the spirit of faith.
By reason I see a thing is so;
by faith I know it as it is.
I have seen thee by reason and have not been amazed,
I have seen thee as thou art in thy Son
and have been ravished to behold thee.

—Old Puritan prayer

16

Fix your eyes on Jesus
for motivation

I was plodding along in the early stages of this book, semi-satisfied with the bulk of the work thus far—the usual stack of yellow sheets written in longhand.

I knew much of it was secondhand, the results of lots of reading and study and putting down thoughts of my own—but also heavily laced with quotes.

A little of it was good; most of it just lay there. Well, it was six months to the publisher's deadline; I figured with time something would come together.

God knew what I needed: a K.I.T.P. (That's short for "kick in the pants.")

Jolt One: I asked Ray to critique something else I'd written. "It's too borrowed," said Ray. "It's not enough *you*."

Oh, my. This new book manuscript (which he hadn't seen yet) was even more borrowed.

Jolt Two: A woman I'd never met wrote saying she was praying for my new book and wanted to give me a verse in connection with it: 1 John 1:1.

Oh, my goodness!—

> That which . . . we have heard [wrote John], which we have seen with our eyes, which we have looked at and our hands have touched—this we proclaim concerning the Word of Life.

My eyes, really for the first time since beginning to work on Fix Your Eyes on Jesus, *fixed on Him!* (So far they'd been fixed on my project.)

I looked up in surprise.

He seemed to be telling me, "Anne, you've gone about this all wrong. Your gift isn't enough. Your experience isn't enough. Your usual formula for the bookwriting process isn't enough.

"All gathered human resources, in themselves, are a Tower of Babel; they're impotent. *Without Me you can do nothing*.

"Fix your eyes again on Me. Listen to My fresh directions."

And so I "listened" to 1 John 1:1, from Him:

1. To be authentic, the book must come from what I myself have seen and heard and felt—from my own experiences and knowledge, not just other people's passed on (don't bottle-feed, breast-feed!)—

> That which [you] have heard, which [you] have seen with [your] eyes . . . this . . . proclaim."

2. And yet it mustn't be primarily about *me*:

This . . . proclaim *concerning the Word of Life.*

I was ablaze! I'd received my K.I.T.P. I knew how to go.

Look, at the moment are you just plodding, too? Don't lose heart.

My six months of going through the motions weren't worthless; *uninspired work is better than no work at all.* I'd gotten a little good material, and most of all it made me so grateful at last for that fresh voice from the Lord.

But *are you,* as I was, *in the plodding stage*—doing what you think you're supposed to do, but without fire, without strong motivation, without a fresh sense of direction?

Or are you operating primarily off your own personality, your training, your particular expertise? Are you—even as a Christian—living basically on the human level?

Or are you only drawing on yesterday? Are you eating moldy manna? Are you stale?

In other words, *do you need a new K.I.T.P.?*

Fix your eyes on Jesus. In Deuteronomy 1: 6 and 7, He says to you,

> You have stayed long enough at this mountain. Break camp and advance.

17

Fix your eyes on Jesus
for consistency

Fixing your eyes on Jesus doesn't mean concentrating on Him so diligently that you eventually collapse from exhaustion.

Even when a person's job demands momentary total absorption, he can still love his marriage partner with great steadiness and consistence. And your relationship with the Lord is the same: The continuity of your life will be a matter first of heart, of unchanging purpose, of unswerving direction.

Continuity is essential for anything: any good work of art, any good project, any good life. Once you've fixed your eyes on Jesus, let there start to be about you a sense of consistency, reliability, unbrokenness.

> My eyes are ever on the Lord (Psalm 25:15).

It's the way Jesus is—"the same yesterday and today and forever" (Hebrews 13:8). And *He continually has His eye fixed on you.*

- *His eyes continually saw your past:*
  "You created my inmost being:
  > you knit me together in my mother's womb.
  Your eyes saw my unformed body" (Psalm 139:13, 16).

- *His eyes continually see your present:*
  "The eyes of the Lord are on the righteous,
  > and his ears are attentive to their cry" (Psalm 34:15).

- *His eyes continually see your future:*
  "He does not take his eyes off the righteous;
  > he enthrones them with kings
  > and exalts them forever" (Job 36:7).

Oh, how steady, how consistent, how reliable is your Lord Jesus!
His love is unchanging (Jeremiah 31:3).
His Word is unchanging (1 Peter 1: 24–25).
His throne is unchanging (Hebrews 1:8).
His salvation is unchanging (Hebrews 7: 24–25).
His gifts to you are unchanging (James 1:17).
He Himself is unchanging (Malachi 3:6).

And you want to be like Jesus.

Do you sense that your life has a steadiness to it, a continuity, a consistency? Or do you want it to?

What is it about your life that's up-and-down?

Your weight? Join Weight Watchers or some other group to hold you accountable.

Your affection for your marriage partner, roommate, someone else close? Ask a steady, older, godly person to disciple you. Meet with that one regularly, confess your problem, solicit prayer, and report each time how you're doing.

Your emotions? Get a physical checkup, telling your doctor your specific symptoms.

Your Bible reading and prayer life? Join a small group (four to eight people) to whom you can answer. Ask to be checked up on.

Wherever in yourself you sense a tendency to instability, quickly reach to an outside source and deliberately build in consistency.

The point is, *begin to mold your life to His;* start to reflect Him. "Seek his face always" (Psalm 105:4).

Soon—sooner than you expect—you, too, will begin to project His kind of wonderful

> reliability,
> flow,
> steadiness,
> dependability,
> continuity.

"Continue in the grace of God"! (Acts 13:43)
"Continue in his kindness"! (Romans 11:22)
"Continue in your faith"! (Colossians 1:23)
"Continue to live in him"! (Colossians 2:6)
"Continue in faith, love and holiness"! (1 Timothy 2:15)
"Continue in what you have learned"! (2 Timothy 3:14)
"Continue in him"! (1 John 2:28)

Fix your eyes on Jesus. Then you can sing,

> Moment by moment I'm kept in His love;
> Moment by moment I've life from above;
> Looking to Jesus till glory doth shine—
> Moment by moment, O Lord, I am Thine.

Let's pray together.

O Lord, make me a steady person, focusing on the One who delivers 'my soul from death, my eyes from tears, and my feet from stumbling' (Psalm 116:8).
You will establish, strengthen, settle me. You will hold me firm, O Abba Father. You will make Proverbs 4: 25 and 27 come true for me:

> "Let [my] eyes look straight ahead,
>   fix [my] gaze directly before [me]. . . .
> Do not [let me] swerve to the right or the left."

I trust You for this. *I fix my eyes on You.* In Jesus' name, amen.

"Moment by Moment, " words by Daniel W. White; music by May Whittle Moody.

18

Fix your eyes on Jesus
for continual fellowship with Him

The first night I was a pastor's wife I practically didn't go to bed.

Ray and the three babies and I had moved from Princeton Seminary in New Jersey to our first pastorate in Christiana, Pennsylvania, a town with eleven hundred souls counting absolutely everybody.

You know how moving is.

The children were finally bedded down, Buddy and Margie in their cribs and Sherry on a mattress on the floor. Then the doorbell rang, and a sad-looking lady stood there. Her mother was dying, and she didn't want to care for her alone. Would I come help?

I went to Mrs. Thompson's house. We slept in snatches, but much of the time it seemed we were trying to pry mother's teeth apart to get down pills with teaspoons of water. In the morning I went home again to our new house, a little shaky in the legs.

Was this how it was to be a pastor's wife? Would people call on me every night to help the dying? (Mrs. Thompson's mother died later that morning, and nobody has ever asked me to do that since.)

But there was a special wonder to that first full day in the ministry. I was groggy, but I asked the Lord for His presence to be my strength, and I lived it in living color. *Life was precious. Death was a reality. Somebody had truly needed me and been truly helped.*

The presence of the Lord was all around me, cheering me, reassuring me. I was so aware of His hand on me, His guidance, His mercy.

Perhaps He made it rough on me that first twenty-four hours so that I would early on begin to *fix my eyes on Him* and discover His nearness, His availability. . . .

Maybe you're saying, "Be practical, Anne. *How do I get this habit of being continually aware of Him?"*

Well, I'm still learning myself, but I do have two suggestions.

First, ask Him. I know what I do when left to myself: I'm "prone to wander—Lord, I feel it!—prone to leave the God I love." *Ask Him.* He loves you to.

Second, cooperate with Him. Vote against your natural waywardness! Keep prompting yourself, to form the habit.

Ray writes "PTP" (Practice the Presence) on sticky papers and plasters them on his dashboard, desk, mirror.

If he feels he's really forgetting too much, he sets his wristwatch alarm to go off every fifteen minutes.

I know a housewife who's conditioned herself to remember the Lord whenever she walks through her kitchen door.

I know a working gal who hears Westminster chimes every fifteen minutes from a nearby city clock, and she sings with it her own words: "I love You, Lord; Lord, You are here. . . ."

And when you're conscious of Him, what do you do?

Talk. "Pray continually," says 1 Thessalonians 5:17:
> "Help me in what I'm doing right now. . . ."
> "I love You, Lord. . . ."
> "Forgive me. . . ."
> "Bless the person I'm talking to. . . ."

Catch the flavor of Nehemiah's inner habit:

> The king said to me, "What is it you want?"
> Then I prayed to the God of heaven, and I answered the
> king . . . (Nehemiah 2: 4–5).

Or again,

> All Judah brought the tithes of grain, new wine and oil into
> the storerooms. I put [certain men] in charge. . . . Remember
> me for this, O my God (Nehemiah 13:12–14).

*It's the happiest, most comfortable life possible, keeping a run-
ning conversation going with Him. He loves it, you love it.*

Think of a sponge plunged into the ocean. It soaks up the sea
water until it's totally saturated. Yet—it's still a sponge.

Think of yourself, fixing your eyes on Jesus. You're plunged into
an awareness of His presence, surrounding you wherever you
go. You "soak up" the Lord and all His characteristics until
you're saturated. And yet you're still you.

But this habit doesn't just "happen." *It begins with desire, and
it continues with discipline.* It's not just automatic, it's *learned*—like
somebody's being initiated into a fraternity or sorority, until
they're at last in the fellowship:

> Blessed are those who have learned to acclaim you,
>> who walk in the light of your presence, O Lord.
> They rejoice in your name all the day long;
>> they exult in your righteousness.
> For you are their glory and strength (Psalm 89:15–17).

The ocean becomes the sponge's very own wateriness and saltiness.

The Lord becomes *your very own* glory and strength. You receive all your achievements, your happiness, your wellbeing from what is continually surrounding you: the presence of God Himself. You're soaking Him up!

Then start right now. And check in ten minutes from now, and ten minutes after that. . . . *The presence of God in your life will become your glory and your strength.*

Moses insisted on it (Exodus 33:15).

David wouldn't live without it (Psalm 27:8).

> If you don't have this glory and this strength, my friend, then you're pretty much like any other wife or bank teller or mother or corporation employee or whatever. It's either the presence of God in your life—
>
> > purifying
> > empowering
> > continual
>
> —or else it's just you alone trying to do the best you can. And that just doesn't make it.

Does the thought of practicing His presence seem burdensome to you? Do a bird's wings weigh it down?

Do yourself a favor.

Do your emotions a favor.

Do your physical body a favor:

Fix your eyes continually on Jesus.

Maybe the reason angels live forever is because their eyes are always on Him.

Prayer:

Lord, as I keep reading this book, may I be most conscious
neither of Anne Ortlund nor of myself; may I be most conscious of You. Keep me looking at You, Lord. Teach me—by
means of these words or in spite of these words; may the
teaching come primarily from You.

Throughout the reading of the book, Lord, and then
afterwards when I move on to other things, may I be a
sponge in sea water, soaking You up! Help me to maintain
the habit, both now and in the future. *Keep my eyes fixed on
You!* In Your name, amen.

Never separate yourself from God.
How sweet it is
to live always near those who love us!
—Gold Dust

19

Fix your eyes on Jesus
for a daily "quiet time"

Cartoon seen recently:

A fellow is listening uncertainly as a recorded voice says out of his telephone receiver, "Your number cannot be completed as dialed. Please check the number you are calling and dial again. Or ask yourself if talking to another person is what you really need at this moment!"

Sometimes your need is just to be quiet.

At least once a day, you need to back off from all the other voices and hear only His. It needs to be a long enough time to be meaningful—to express your love, confess your sins, receive guidance, delight in Him, *listen.*

I have an electric toothbrush, and I don't take it with me to conferences because it needs frequent plugging into the socket to get re-juiced. And you and I can't go anywhere for very long without the sacrifice of times of quiet with God to get restored again.

I said *sacrifice*.

A thirty-ish woman said to me at a conference two days ago, "There's no way I can have a daily quiet time. I have five small children who take everything I've got, and then I work every day from four to midnight." As I questioned her, I discovered she has a working husband and almost no debts.

She stood there, weepy, overweight, defeated. It would mean true sacrifice for her to add time with the Lord to her exhausting days. But *until she does, she may not hear His solutions and so she'll spiral ever farther downward.*

Whatever your circumstances—if you'd lived in Old Testament times you would have regularly given God a male animal or bird—whatever you could afford—*that had no defects: something you'd humanly want or even "need" for yourself.*

If you're stressed out from a tight schedule, offer God the sacrifice of your time.

If you love to be with people, give Him the sacrifice of your solitude.

If you're not very excited yet about Bible reading and prayer, lift up to Him the sacrifice of your surrendered will.

And when you sit down or kneel to be with Him, what do you do?

No two people will have quiet times just alike, but first decide on a time, a place, and a plan—and stick to it.

Since the children were in school, except when I'm conference speaking, I've chosen mid-mornings—my high-energy time. I have with me my Bible, my notebook, and a pen.

First, in the prayer section of my notebook, I put the date and I write that day's prayers to Him. Maybe I should read my Bible first for a while. . . . Anyway, this is my current habit.

I write out my prayers to Him in complete sentences, like writing to a friend. Sometimes I structure sections of my prayer to ACTS: *adoration, confession, thanksgiving,* and *supplication.* That keeps me from getting the "gimme's" too much.[1]

In any case, writing my prayers has probably been the greatest single encouragement in my walk with the Lord! Practically, it keeps my mind from wandering, and it monitors how much time each day I'm actually giving Him in undistracted prayer—so I can't fool myself.

The Big Bonus has been discovering how seriously God takes my requests! Weeks or months later I've looked back and read over earlier prayers, and been amazed to see how He's started the wheels of heaven turning to bring about the things I asked of Him!

Then I take up His Word, still with notebook and pen in hand.[2]

For years Ray and I have read straight through the Bible annually. Of course, any way you read through God's Word will bring blessing—but this is what I said to my eager young friend Cathy the other day. I urged her not to dip from Old Testament to New Testament to Psalms and back again. I said that's like trying to explore a mountain by being blindfolded and helicoptered into one section and studying that; then being blindfolded again and helicoptered into another section and studying that. . . .

The Bible is a *book.* It goes from start to finish, unfolding stories and developing themes as it goes. *Get the sweep of the whole, over and over!* Five pages a day will do it in a year.

Oh, how I love my personal Bible! It's brown, of course (smile). Each year in the margins I write comments and jot in cross-references and write brief prayers concerning what I'm reading, with the date beside it. Then each year I come to those roadmarks again. My Bible represents my personal walk with

---

[1] For more helps on private prayer and Bible reading, see my book *Disciplines of the Beautiful Woman,* pages 71–73 and 118–22.

[2] If you're interested in acquiring a notebook, write me. Ray and I have put together for others, at minimum cost, the same kind of notebook that we use. Our address is at the back of this book.

God for a period of three or four years, and when it's filled and ragged I start another.

Right now I'm finishing up the fourth year with this beloved, tattered old Bible, and because the Exodus 13–14 page is detached, the Israelites are having trouble getting across the Red Sea.

They keep wandering off onto my lap.

Let's pray together:

Lord, I need more prayer and more of Your Word in my life! Show me how to schedule these and how to structure them, to be diligent, consistent, making progress. Guide me to the right helps.

My problem is desire, Lord! *Stir me up, O Holy Spirit of God.* Help me to thirst for, to crave the pure milk of Your Word (1 Peter 2:2). It's what I need, what those around me need, what the world needs. And as I flood it with prayer, it will help me grow in grace as well as in knowledge (2 Peter 3:18).

Lord, I consecrate myself to You for this. In myself I will fail, but *I fix my eyes on You.*

In Christ's lovely name, amen.

Prayer . . . indicates to God that
someone would speak to Him, and God, so
good and gracious, is ever ready to listen
(with all reverence we say it) with the prompt
attention of a faithful servant.

—Gold Dust

20

Fix your eyes on Jesus
for serving Him

Why do you do voluntary service?

Because you enjoy it?

Because it makes you a better person?

Because it pleases your pastor or your spouse or someone else?

Because you feel you need to pitch in and do your share?

There were "church workers" called Levites in Ezekiel 44 whom God *exposed* as serving for the reasons above!

They had their eyes on themselves and on others, but not on Him.

This particular group of Levites had had a long history of serving themselves and other people—to the point of even helping others in their idol worship! (Correct doctrine isn't too important to you when you get carried away wanting to please other people.)

And God said, "All right, from now on just please people, not Me. You weren't focused on Me before; from now on I won't *allow* you to be. You can keep on doing church 'busy work,' but I won't let you minister to Me Myself."

It makes all the difference.

An eye fixed on self is full of confusion: "How much commitment is commitment? If I teach a Sunday school class can I never go away weekends? If I join the choir, what happens when choir practice night comes and I'm exhausted?"

The "me generation" says, "I can only be somewhat committed to you because I'm first committed to me."

> [A man] said, "I will follow you, Lord, but first let me go
> back and say goodbye to my family."
> Jesus replied, "No one who puts his hand to the plow and
> looks back is fit for the kingdom of God" (Luke 9: 61–62).

But fix your eyes on Jesus, and you yourself will be helped the most.

An eye fixed on service to others is full of politics, and the service is performed in

> bossiness
> fussiness
> competition
> criticalness
> selfwill
> ego

But fix your eyes on Jesus, and others will be helped the most.

You have access to the Lord Himself! Don't stop short in the vestibule.

Are you a "ministry-centered" person? You'll get depleted, irritated and abrasive, exhausted.

Are you a "Christ-centered" person? Even as you serve Him, you'll stay nourished, happy, rested.

Fix your eyes on Jesus!

Let's talk to Him about our service—I, Anne Ortlund, and you, too—through an old Puritan prayer:

"O my Lord,
Forgive me for serving thee in sinful ways—
        by glorying in my own strength,
        by forcing myself to minister through necessity,
        by accepting the applause of others,
        by trusting in assumed grace and spiritual affection,
        by a faith that rests on my hold on Christ,
            not on him alone. . . .
Help me to see
        that it is faith stirred by grace that does the deed . . .
        that faith centers in thee as God all-sufficient,
            Father, Son, Holy Spirit . . .
If I have not such faith I am nothing. . . .
Keep me in a faith that works by love,
                and serves by grace." Amen.

21

Fix your eyes on Jesus
for a job well done

You've come to the end of a project, and it's turned out smashing.

You put on this year's mother-daughter banquet, and everyone says it was the best ever.

Or you headed your church's building project, and there the building stands now, in all its glory.

Or you've turned out great kids, or you've made a name for yourself in your career.

Or maybe you're still in midstream—in your marriage, your job, your parenting—but it's going better than you ever dreamed.

Don't fix your eyes on yourself.

1. Don't exalt yourself. In Isaiah 42:8 the Lord absolutely thunders, "I will not share my glory with another."

2. But also, don't demean yourself. Don't say, "It wasn't anything; He's everything, I'm nothing." Talking that way sounds as if you want everyone to protest, "Oh, no, you're wonderful!"

Fix your eyes on Jesus.

He also did a great job—infinitely greater than yours. And now the Achiever has allowed you, too, to experience the thrill of achievement. Identify with Him!

On the cross He said a special word: in the Greek, *"Tetelestai."* We translate it "It is finished." It didn't mean "I give up; I quit"—it was a great cry of triumph: "I did it! I really did it!"

According to Bible scholar F.W. Boreham, that word was—

> A cattleman's word, for instance. When his cow produced a calf seemingly healthy and without blemish, the rancher might exclaim, *"Tetelestai!"*
>
> Or an artist's word. When a painter finished a work and stepped back and examined it critically and could find nothing more to be done, he could announce, *"Tetelestai."*

Jesus said that word with the last breath of His life. He said it in great pain, and yet with a sense of great accomplishment.

Your achievement, too, is bittersweet; you went through a lot. There were pitfalls along the way, but He enabled you and the job turned out great.

You can understand His feelings, at least a little. And He understands yours.

Savor the thrill: *"Tetelestai!"*

Squeeze the juices out of your relief and your delight.

And think about Jesus: *"Tetelestai!"* Enjoy with Him *His* relief and delight!

And worship Him.

Why don't you pray to Him right now:

Dear Lord Jesus, I don't fix my eyes on this achievement; it was for You.
I don't want to call attention to myself in all this; I don't want either to exalt myself or to belittle myself.
O Lord, I lay my crown at Your feet. Alleluia!
Amen.

22

Fix your eyes on Jesus
for pure pleasure

Have you thought about what awesome and exquisite *fun* is possible, the more you fix your eyes on Jesus?

You understand more and more

    His love

    His compassion

    His grace and His graciousness to *you*.

And you begin to realize just how forgiven and how eagerly received by Him you really are!

So many Christians live essentially apart from Him—officially connected but not enjoying Him at all. They stay aloof because they don't understand *what He's really like*.

Think of it this way.

The fabulous Groom, the ultimate "catch," marries His bride.

But thereafter, desolate, she wanders the city streets—not understanding that He has a home waiting for her, every provision for her needs, a great life together of both purpose and joy, and His own faithful, loving arms.

Maybe because of her own low self-image and guilt complex, she spends her time in bars and sleeping around, convinced her Husband couldn't possibly like her or want her.

Or maybe, remembering how wonderful He was at the wedding, she thinks if she could just shape up she could win His affection. So she lives a life of grim asceticism—totally misunderstanding what kind of Man it was she married (Luke 7: 33–34).

But whether she lives in license or legalisms, she lives far from her Husband's dear presence. She never moves into His home and His heart and has a ball!

It makes you want to cry.

It makes *Him* want to cry, too, because it's so unnecessary. He'd written her a wonderful letter explaining just how much He loves her and how much pleasure He has waiting for her. But either she doesn't bother to read it, or else the good parts of the letter just seem too good to be true.

Christian, let me describe to you what the letter says it's like, if you'll repent of your distance and confess your sins and move in and live close to Jesus:

> [Believers] are led in with joy and gladness;
> They enter the presence of the king (Psalm 45:15).

> In [his] presence is fullness of joy;
> at [his] right hand there are pleasures for evermore (Psalm 16:11, KJV).

> You have made [the believer] glad with the joy of your presence (Psalm 21:6).

And He'll be so happy, too!

> The Lord . . . will take great delight in you,
> he will quiet you with his love,
> he will rejoice over you with singing (Zephaniah 3:17).

And when He's in the company of His dear ones *He loves to party*. That's what He's like!

Moses and the other spiritual leaders of Israel "went up and saw the God of Israel"—gulp!—and "they ate and drank" (Exodus 24: 9–11)!

King David and his people faithfully sacrificed to atone for their sins, and then "they ate and drank with great joy in the presence of the Lord" (1 Chronicles 29: 22).

The prodigal son got sick of his waywardness and repented and came home, and his father provided great new clothes for him, a new ring, and a dinner party with music and dancing (Luke 15: 22–25).

You see, it's only a Christian's own attitude that causes any blockage. When you asked God to forgive you and "save" you (that's a good biblical word)—from that moment on *He doesn't hold anything further against you. He doesn't count your sins against you any more.*

That's the whole reason for the cross.

Jesus did the strongest possible thing—He sacrificed His own life, to produce the strongest possible salvation—He completely exonerated you from your sins.

> Therefore there is now no condemnation for those who are in Christ Jesus (Rom. 8:1)!

If you're a believer—if you're "in Christ"—then kick up your heels! Celebrate the Lord! Celebrate yourself!

> Let all who take refuge in [the Lord] be glad;
> let them ever sing for joy (Psalm 5:11).

> Rejoice in the Lord always. I will say it again: rejoice! (Philippians 4:4).

And Ephesians 1 says twice that God's will and pleasure go together (verses 5 and 9)!

Discover what J.I. Packer says are the marks of those who really get to know the Lord: they have "gaiety, goodness, and an unfetteredness of spirit"!

They say the missionary to India called "Praying Hyde" was known for two things: the deep commitment of his prayer life and the hilarity of his laugh!

> "He who is enslaved to the compass has the freedom of the sea."

Fix your eyes steadfastly on Jesus—and discover a life of pleasure you never dreamed possible.

Why don't you pray to Him:

Lord, the challenge of Your presence is that it's so purifying . . . but why should I want to stay weighted down with sins, and far from You?

With fresh confession of my sins and with humility and awe I come close.

"Let the hearts of those who seek the Lord rejoice" (Psalm 105:3).

Lord, You are wonderful! In Jesus' name, amen.

"It is very pleasant to live here in our beautiful world. My eyes cannot see the beautiful things, but my mind can see them all, and so I am joyful all the day."

—So said blind and deaf Helen Keller.

Fix your eyes on Jesus.

23

Fix your eyes on Jesus in your living

Parts of your life will be good, maybe even wonderful.

Parts of your life will be bad, maybe awful.

Don't fix your eyes too much on any of it. If you look too much at the good you'll get cocky. If you look too much at the bad you'll get defeated. Anyway, what's good today may be bad tomorrow, and what's bad today may be wonderful tomorrow.

Nowhere does the Bible say to put your hope in life improvement; you'd spend your days in fear of disappointment.

Hope in God. Fix your eyes on Him, and let Him give you what He wants to; *for you it will all turn out to be good.*

I get such a kick out of reading the old Christian classics. The truths don't change, but the terms do.

One seventeenth-century writer was commenting about people who came back to his area of Europe from visiting Peru. He says of course they brought back gold and silver, but they were also apt to bring apes and parrots—"because they neither cost much, nor are burdensome"! (Can you believe it? I don't know, I think traveling with apes might be burdensome, but I must be a sissy.)

And so, he continues, when good things happen to you, accept them like parrots and apes—enjoy them—"provided they don't cost [you] too much care and attention, nor involve [you] in trouble, anxiety, disputes or contentions"!

(I can see the possibility of apes causing anxiety.)

His point is, don't let nice things in your life distract you from fixing your eyes on Jesus.

(This sage from long ago also suggests that if you *really* get elevated, try to accept what comes from your admirers "with prudence and discretion, accompanied by charity and suavity of manners"! Does that strike you as funny, too? Whatever good things come, don't forget to be suave!)

But through the centuries God's wise ones emphasize the same thing: "fix your eyes, fix your eyes."

William Law said around 1750 that everyone fixes their eyes on something; he interpreted that as "praying without ceasing." He said people pray continually as long as they're alive, because it's part of human nature.

> The [person] whose heart habitually tends toward the riches, honors, powers or pleasures of this life, is in a continual state of prayer toward all these things. His spirit stands always bent towards them. They have his hope, his love, his faith, and are . . . in reality the God of his heart."[1]

Can't you see that whatever we think is lacking or in short supply in our life, we could easily "pray without ceasing" toward that?

in a jail cell, pray without ceasing toward release
in poverty, pray toward money

---

[1] William Law, *A Serious Call to a Devout and Holy Life*, p. 155.

under an oppressive government, toward freedom
in loneliness, toward companionship. . . .

All the milling peoples of the world, each lacking *something*,
can fix their eyes on their particular lack and be always restless,
complaining, ungrateful, unhappy.

I'm speaking to myself as well. *In your good times, in your
bad times, when life is wonderful, when life is awful—don't fix
your eyes on your life.*

Fix your eyes on Jesus.

This was the little gem on my "Keswick calendar" recently:

> "Live while you live," the epicure would say,
> "And seize the pleasures of the present day."
>> "Live while you live," the faithful preacher cries,
>> "And give to God each moment as it flies."
> Lord, in my view, let each united be:
> I live in pleasure while I live for Thee.[2]

I'm writing more than I've attained, but it both motivates
me and stabilizes me to read this other quotation from that same
remarkable William Law, written also around 1750:

> The pious soul that eyes only God . . . can have no stop in
> its progress; light and darkness equally assist him.
> In the light he looks up to God. In the darkness he lays hold
> of God, and so they both do him the same good.[3]

---

[2] P. Doddridge, "Keswick Calendar," Friday, December 14, 1990.

[3] William Law, *A Serious Call to a Devout and Holy Life*, p. 159.

Prayer:

O Father! I confess to You I don't yet have a deep conviction in my heart that darkness and light are equal.
Lord Jesus Christ! I want to develop before You a "holy carelessness." I have a long way to go, but that phrase makes my mouth water.

Teach me to be without concern concerning all that concerns me!—knowing that I am totally in Your perfect hands.
Teach me to fix my eyes on You, and to take what You give with poise and gratitude.
Teach me to say with Paul, "I have learned to be content whatever the circumstances. I know what it is to be in need, and I know what it is to have plenty. I have learned the secret of being content in any and every situation . . ." (Philippians 4:12).
Teach me that secret, Lord Jesus.
I fix my eyes on You. Amen.

Let us fix our eyes on Jesus . . .
  that He may cast us down, and that He may raise us up;
  that He may afflict us, and that He may comfort us;
  that He may despoil us, and that He may enrich us;
  that He may teach us to pray, and that He may answer our prayers;
  that while leaving us in the world, He may separate us from it,
    our life being hidden with Him in God,
    and our behaviour bearing witness to Him before men.

—Theodore Monod,
early twentieth century

24

Fix your eyes on Jesus
in your dying

I was listening yesterday to the "Haven of Rest" radio broadcast. My favorite keyboardist, Duane Condon, was accompanying magnificently, and one of my favorite singers, bass Glenn Shoemaker, was singing "Guide Me, O Thou Great Jehovah."

(I listen to "Haven," on which Ray is the speaker, every morning at eight. I do things before and after, but at eight I turn on the little bathroom radio and dress and put on my face while I'm listening.)

Duane and Glenn came to verse three, and their music became slower, more majestic, and charged with triumphant exhilaration:

> When I tread the verge of Jordan,
> Bid my anxious fears subside;
> Death of Death and hell's Destruction
> [What magnificent names for Christ!]

> Land me safe on Canaan's side;
> Songs of praises, songs of praises
> I will ever give to Thee!

I thought of my precious friend Becky, in my small group of disciples last year, who just the day before had died of cancer, barely thirty years old. I leaned into the mirror to put cover-up on some wrinkles. And though I love her and I miss her already, I thought, *"You lucky rascal, Becky! You beat me there."*

I remember Ray preaching one time about Lazarus dying and his sisters' grief and Jesus raising Lazarus again. With tongue in cheek, Ray described the scene:

Lazarus is up in heaven. He's been there four days, and it's fantastic. He's gotten his robe and his golden shoes and they've already started him on his harp lessons.

Then he gets the news.

"Lazarus, you gotta go back."

"What? *Go back?* No way. . . . Why?"

"The girls want you."

Lazarus groans. "The girls? You gotta be kidding. . . . Do I have to go?"

He finally gets persuaded, and he starts taking off his golden shoes. He hangs his robe and his harp in the locker he's been assigned, and he says, "Fellas, don't touch those things, my name's on them. And look, I'll be back!"

And he struggles back into his lousy old grave wrappings. . . .

If we had any idea how wonderful the next life is, we wouldn't hang onto this one so tenaciously!

Of course the pain of losing loved ones—though temporarily— is real enough. We don't "grieve like the rest of men, who have no hope" (1 Thessalonians 4:13), *but we do grieve*—sometimes terribly, deeply, excruciatingly in our loss.

But as far as death goes, we can be absolutely light-hearted. We've been freed from all fear of it (Hebrews 2:15); it has no more victory over us, no sting (1 Corinthians 15:55).

That wonderful Twenty-third Psalm says,

> Even though I walk
> > through the valley of the shadow of death,
> I will fear no evil.

If a truck runs over you, you can get really ruined.

If the *shadow* of a truck runs over you, what happens?

Psalm 23 speaks only of your walking through the *shadow* of death. . . . *Is that all?*

In your thinking about dying, get Jesus' perspective.

And when your own time comes to die, *fix your eyes on Him.*

> "Stephen, full of the Holy Spirit, looked up to heaven [the King James Version says 'looked up steadfastly'] and saw the glory of God, and Jesus standing at the right hand of God.
>
> "'Look,' he said, 'I see heaven open. . . .'
> "Then . . . he fell asleep" (Acts 7: 55–56, 60).

> When the waters are rough and the sky is dark, look towards the shore; the lights shining there will attract and encourage you. Stephen saw those lights. . . .
>
> There, where his Savior was, was his destination, his home, and from thence came the grace and power that carried him through.[1]

Fix your eyes on Jesus!

---

[1] Clifford Lewis, "Keswick Calendar", Tuesday, January 15, 1991.

Why don't you sing this song to Him?

Precious Lord, take my hand, lead me on, help me stand;
    I am tired, I am weak, I am worn;
Through the storm, through the night, lead me on to the light;
    Take my hand, precious Lord, lead me home.

When my way grows drear, precious Lord, linger near,
    When my life is almost gone;
Hear my cry, hear my call, hold my hand lest I fall:
    Take my hand, precious Lord, lead me home.

When the darkness appears and the night draws near,
    And the day is past and gone,
At the river I stand, guide my foot, hold my hand,
    Take my hand, precious Lord, lead me home.[2]

---

[2] Thomas Dorsey, 1938. Copyright 1938 Hill and Range Songs, Inc. Copyright received, assigned to Unichappell Music, Inc. (Rightson Music, publisher). Used by permission of Hal Leonard Corporation.

Looking unto Jesus (Hebrews 12:2).
Only three little words,
but in those three little words
is the whole secret of life.
—Theodore Monod,
early twentieth century

PART 3

Fix your eyes on Jesus
to get biblical understanding

25

Fix your eyes on Jesus
to fix your eyes on Jesus

Everything you learn about Jesus Christ, as you look and look, is so magnificent that you could never adequately explain Him to anyone else.

A tribesman once "fixed his eyes" for the first time on the ocean. He was flabbergasted! He got a quart jar to take some back so he could show his people.

Jesus Christ is "the radiance of God's glory and the exact representation of his being" (Hebrews 1:3), "the exact likeness of the unseen God" (Colossians 1:15, TLB).

> No angel in the sky
> Can fully bear that sight,
> But downward bends his wond'ring eye
> At mysteries so bright.[1]

---

[1] Matthew Bridges: "Crown Him with Many Crowns."

But though angels may look down, God commands you in Hebrews 12:2 to gaze studiously at Jesus, this One who is the very "radiance" of God's glory.

Fix your eyes on Him.

Look at what you're looking at.

You've looked through a toy kaleidoscope, and as you twisted the tube, the bits of colored glass kept changing patterns over and over. Look at Jesus Christ to see God's glory, and that glory will be "new every morning," always different, always beautiful.

"Show me your glory," Moses begged the Lord God.

"No man can see my face and live," said God. "But I will put you in a cleft of [a certain] rock and cover you with my hand until I have passed by. Then I will remove my hand and you will see my back" (Exodus 33:22–23). (His *back?* Moses had asked to see His *glory.* God is so mysterious.)

When God put Moses there in the rock, what was the glory of God that He allowed Moses to see?

He "saw" a proclamation of His name—that God is

> The LORD, the LORD,
> the compassionate and gracious God,
> slow to anger,
> abounding in love and faithfulness,
> maintaining love to thousands,
> and forgiving wickedness, rebellion and sin.
> Yet he does not leave the guilty unpunished . . . (Exodus 34:6–7).

You're looking through the kaleidoscope at Jesus Christ, "the radiance of God's glory." Twist the tube a little.

Oh—*He's the* LORD, transfigured before Peter, James, and John. His face shines like the sun, and His clothes become as white as the light. . . . Twist the tube.

Oh—*He is the compassionate God.* Two blind men are before Him, begging, "Lord, we want our sight." And Jesus touches their eyes and they see. . . . Twist the tube.

Look: *He's not leaving the guilty unpunished.* He's found moneychangers in the temple; He's made a whip out of cords, and He's overturning their tables and driving them out! . . . Twist the tube.

"Abounding in love and faithfulness:" Now He's feeding five thousand hungry people. Twist. . . .

"Gracious:" He's taking children into His arms. Twist. . . .

"Forgiving wickedness:" He's groaning from the cross, "Father, forgive them. . . ."
Keep twisting and twisting, and every time you stop, you'll see another radiant facet of the glory of God.

And yet all this, so far, is only His back! *What will be the rest of God's glory, which will be revealed when you see His face?!*

Prayer:

O Lord Jesus, because You are all-important, all-worthy, I press on to fix my eyes on You! In Your incomparable name, amen.

26

Fix your eyes on Jesus
as seen in the Bible

I remember ministering with Ray in Brazil and being in utter fatigue. In between meetings I'd lie on the bed and think, "I absolutely cannot get up again."

Then in my through-the-Bible daily reading I came to 2 Chronicles 15:7:

> But as for you, be strong and do not give up, for your work will be rewarded.

That day *God gave that verse just to me*—and I received it. And it was wonderful! I literally had all the pep I needed. In less than ten days we were ministering in Japan, and I was bouncing with energy.

And not that I couldn't—but so far I've never felt that deep fatigue again.

Later on that same Brazil trip, on a plane flying in the interior, I sat by a bright-faced young guy with a Bible. We had no common language at all, but I showed him on my page my wonderful new verse. He looked it up in his Portuguese Bible and glowed. Then he pointed out another page in his Bible, and I looked up that one:

> Stand firm. Let nothing move you. Always give yourselves fully to the work of the Lord, because you know that your labor in the Lord is not in vain (1 Corinthians 15:58).

And on we went, swapping marvelous verses and fellowshiping together. What a thrill! We parted with a hug.

There is no book like this book—for two reasons.
First, from cover to cover, it reveals Jesus Christ, so you can look long and intimately at Him.

You know the New Testament is about Him; it was written after His life, death, and resurrection. But the Old Testament was written centuries before; is that about Him, too?

"Absolutely," said Jesus.

These are the scriptures that testify about me (John 5:39).

Take a look.

In the Old Testament's very first book God promised Abraham,

> For all the land which thou seest, to thee will I give it, and to thy seed forever (Genesis 13:15, KJV).

And two thousand years later in the New Testament, the Spirit of God explains that He was talking back there about Jesus Christ:

> He saith not, "and to seeds," as of many, but as one, "and to thy seed," which is Christ (Galatians 3:16, KJV).

Here's Psalm 110:1, written a thousand years before Jesus:

> The LORD says to my Lord:
> "Sit at my right hand
> until I make your enemies
> a footstool for your feet."

Jesus said this verse referred to Himself (Mark 12: 35–37). It was Jehovah speaking to Adonai—the Father speaking to the Son.

And Peter, preaching on Pentecost in Acts 2 said the Psalms of David talked about Jesus of Nazareth.

And Hebrews 1:8 says Psalm 45: 6–7 refers to Jesus.

And around 750 B.C. the prophet Isaiah wrote,

> I saw the Lord seated on a throne, high and exalted,
> and the train of his robe filled the temple (Isaiah 6:1).

What an awesome sight!

And John reveals whom he saw: the preexistent Christ. "Isaiah . . . saw Jesus' glory" (John 12:41).

You see,

> "The New is in the Old contained;
> The Old is by the New explained."

From Genesis to Revelation *Jesus is there,* and *if you want to fix your eyes on Him, you must look at His entire book.*

A.W. Tozer used to say, "Nothing less than a whole Bible can make a whole Christian."[1]

Dr. Donald Grey Barnhouse was an American preacher of the last generation, and nobody ever sparkled when he preached like Dr. Barnhouse.

One time he was telling his audience why they needed to read the whole Bible. He reminded them how God said to Abraham, "I'm going to give you this land (Palestine), so go walk

---

[1] *Still Waters, Deep Waters,* p. 66.

around it. Every place you set your foot will be yours" (loose wording of Genesis 13: 14, 17; Deuteronomy 11:24; and Joshua 1:3).

The way Dr. Barnhouse told it, that evening Abraham took a walk, walking around about an acre—and that night he owned an acre.

The next day he walked around a mile, and he owned the mile.

And when the sheep had grazed there, he took them over to the next valley, and he owned the valley. ("Every place where you set your foot will be yours.")

It wasn't too many years until he owned everything from Dan to Beersheba—just by putting his foot down.

And, said Dr. Barnhouse with his sparkle, lots of Christians possess a very small Bible. They have John 3:16 and the Twenty-third Psalm and a few other little passages, and they keep going back and forth from one to another, maybe grazing those little spots down to bare rock. And that's all they have.

But God says, "Go, walk through the length and breadth of the land! Every place where you set your foot will be yours"—full of wonderful truths just for you.

Take up your Bible; look at it. The land is before you, ready for you to possess.

And *Jesus is there!* "Handle Me, and see," He says (Luke 24:39, KJV).

So read your Bible from cover to cover, for two reasons.[2] *First*, as we said, *because it reveals Jesus Christ to you.*

And *second, because it reveals yourself to you!*

"What?" you're asking. "What do you mean?"

Well, you have to agree, being humans, that we're definitely more curious to read a book about ourselves. The Bible's about Jesus—but it's also about you.

I would think one reason Jesus loved the Old Testament, the Scriptures of His day, is just what we've been saying: because

[2] Ray and I suggest, as a guide, *The Daily Walk*, P.O. Box 478, Mt. Morris, IL 61054.

they were full of Him. In them He saw Himself. And wouldn't they have been a powerful motivation for Him to fulfill everything that He saw written about Himself?

When He felt depleted from healing people (Mark 5:30), what a thrill to remember what Isaiah had predicted:

> Surely he took up our infirmities
> and carried our sorrows (Isaiah 53:4; Matthew 8:17).

When He was physically exhausted from teaching by parables—sometimes to thousands at once with no microphone—how fulfilling to remember that Asaph the musician had sung a psalm that one day He would do just that:

> I will open my mouth in parables,
> I will utter things hidden since the creation of the world
> (Psalm 78:2; Matthew 13: 34–35).

And when He needed "go-power" to face that excruciating cross, how He must have held before His eyes the prophecy,

> He will not falter or be discouraged
> till he establish justice on earth (Isaiah 42:4)!

And *here's a remarkable thing: the Bible not only describes Jesus, it describes you.* His likeness is there—but so is yours. God gives you in His Word a picture of what He means for you to be:

> Completely humble and gentle . . . patient (Ephesians 4:2).
> Strong in the Lord and in his mighty power (Ephesians 6:10).
> Without complaining or arguing (Philippians 2:14).
> Not anxious, guarded by peace (Philippians 4:6–7).
> Forgiving, loving (Colossians 3:13–14).
> Encouraging one another (1 Thessalonians 5:11).
> Respectful of leadership (1 Thessalonians 5:12).
> Always joyful (1 Thessalonians 5:16).
> Continually praying (1 Thessalonians 5:17).

Giving thanks in all circumstances (1 Thessalonians 5:18).
Avoiding every kind of evil (1 Thessalonians 5:22).
Hard working (2 Thessalonians 3:11–13).
Watching for the Lord's return (1 Thessalonians 1:10).
More than conquerors (Romans 8:37)!

So *love the Scriptures*, as Jesus did. Search there for God's picture of your own intended image and likeness, and then seek to fulfill through your own life and personality exactly what you see.

When you fix your eyes on Jesus, as seen in the Bible, you're fixing your eyes on aspects, characteristics of Him that God wants you to have, as well.

Then you will

. . . reflect the Lord's glory, [and be] transformed into his [own] likeness with ever-increasing glory, which comes from the Lord (2 Corinthians 3:18)!

Why don't you kneel where you are, and pray this prayer:

O Lord, what a vision You have set before me! Now give me a heart to pursue this vision, the discipline to fulfill it.

"Beyond the sacred page
I seek Thee, Lord. . . ."

"Open my eyes, that I may see wonderful
things in your law" (Psalm 119:18).

"The commands of the Lord are radiant,
giving light to the eyes" (Psalm 19:8).

Father, as I probe Your Word, *fix my eyes on Jesus,* "the eyes of [my] understanding being enlightened, that [I] may know what is the hope of his calling" (Ephesians 1:18).
In His own dear name, amen.

[Fix your eyes on] Jesus in the Scriptures,
to learn there what He is,
what He has done,
what He gives,
what He desires;
to find in His character our pattern,
in His teachings our instruction,
in His precepts our law,
in His promises our support,
in His person and in His work
a full satisfaction provided for every need of our souls.
—Theodore Monod

27

Fix your eyes on Jesus the Son of Man

The come and go of busy feet
With sound of hammer down the busy street,
A little two-roomed house with scarce a breath
Of air; in busy, crowded Nazareth.
Yes, here for love of thee, through silent years—
    Oh, pause and see, if thou art wise—
The King of Kings dwelt in disguise.[1]

Jesus was indeed the King of Kings—but don't forget He was also a real human being.

Luke the doctor recorded that the Son of God was truly *born*, and wrapped in cloths and placed in a manger (Luke 2:7).

When He was eight days old the baby was circumcised (2:21) and then cuddled in an old man's arms (2:28).

---

[1] Oswald Sanders, *Christ Incomparable*, p. 33.

He grew as a child (2:40, 52), and once as a twelve-year-old He got separated from His parents and scolded (2:41–48), although His reason showed His growing awareness of His specialness and mission (2:49).

As an adult He got hungry (4:2); He shared human sadness (7:13); He liked to eat and drink and socialize with people (7:34). He wasn't omnipresent—He could only be in one place at a time (10:1).

And He died a real death (23:46) and ended His earthly life as He began it: wrapped in cloths and placed not in a manger but a tomb (23: 52–53).

Think about this earthly, human, thirty-three-year life-span.

Jesus spent six times as long working as a carpenter as He did in full-time ministry. He was essentially a blue-collar worker, and that was His identification (Mark 6:3).

And I want to tell you—*it was a good thing He didn't shrink from all those laborious, tedious carpenter-years as His preparation.* Once the ministry began,

> Never in human history were human frame and nervous system to be called on to endure such unremitting strain. . . . Only a physically perfect constitution could have supported such unceasing activity and expenditure of nervous force. . . .
>
> His recorded journeys during the three years covered at least two thousand five hundred miles on foot, frequently surrounded by crowds, and always teaching, preaching, healing.
>
> And what better preparation than twelve hours a day spent in the sawpit or at the bench, planing and hammering? These silent years . . . were invaluable in building up the physical and nervous reserves which were to be so heavily overdrawn in coming days that He would stagger under the weight of His cross.[2]

---

[2] Ibid, pp. 43, 44.

Jesus—pale, puffy-eyed, and effeminate, as in some of our paintings? No way. He was a "man's man."

And since His entrance into this world as a human, He will never cease to be a human!

In His risen manhood He assured the disciples He wasn't a ghost—and He said, "Touch Me and see." And He ate a piece of broiled fish in front of them (Luke 24: 39–42).

Now in heaven there is a Man at the Father's right hand! He's our go-between:

> For there is one God and one mediator between God and men, the man Christ Jesus (1 Timothy 2:5).

He's as manly as ever—*as human as ever*—having become the glorious human that Adam started out to be and lost, and that we soon shall be. He's our prototype! We, too, will be gloriously resurrected,

> And just as we have borne the likeness of the earthly man [Adam], so shall we bear the likeness of the man from heaven [Christ] (1 Corinthians 15:49).

I can hardly wait, can you?

Still, we'll always know the price He paid to get us there. He'll be the only One there with scars in His hands.

Fix your eyes on Jesus—your strong Hero, your Ideal, your Model.

Prayer:

Lord, I look at You, and I discover You're looking at me!

"As in water face answers to face,
    so the heart of one man answers to another"
    (Proverbs 27:19, Berkeley).

You are like me—but perfect. You're all I want to be—but *You're made of my kind of stuff.* I can identify with You; I can move in close and be Your friend.
    What an honor! What a thrill!
    You have said,

"He who walks with the wise grows wise" (Proverbs 13:20).

Lord Jesus Christ, I want to walk with You and grow to be like You. *I fix my eyes on You, my wonderful Companion!* In Your own dear name, amen.

Ecce Homo—see the Man.
Ecce Deum—see your God.
"Veiled in flesh, the Godhead see;
Hail, incarnate Deity"!

28

Fix your eyes on Jesus
the Son of God

There's a very old cartoon by H.T. Webster entitled "Life in Harden County [Illinois] in 1809." It shows two men talking.

"Any news, Ezzie?"

"Squire McClendon's gone down to Washington to see Harding sworn in."

"I hear Bonaparte's trying to subdue Spain."

"New baby boy born down the street at the Lincolns.' Nothin' exciting ever happens around here."

But of course something exciting *had* happened: That new little life would one day reshape American history.

But the first Christmas produced the most dramatic event on earth so far: The Son of God was born on our planet—in a part of His process to reshape all human history from start to finish.

Out of the ivory palaces into a world of woe;
Only His great, eternal love made my Savior go.

He had always, eternally, been alive and active. "In the beginning was the Word," says John 1:1—reaching back beyond creation, before Genesis 1:1!

Just as His death was not the end of Him, so His birth was not the beginning of Him.[1]

He was God. And yet He came to this world and

. . . made himself nothing . . .
being made in human likeness (Philippians 2:6–7).

Incredible! He created everything—and then He voluntarily submitted to His own creation! He became tired and thirsty, just like one of us.

Before, He'd been so furious against sin that He refused at first to lead His people into the promised land: He said they were so rebellious, He "might destroy [them] on the way" (Exodus 33:3).

Yet descending to earth, He stooped so far down that *He meekly asked a prostitute for a drink of water.*

Truly, profoundly, *"He humbled himself"* (Philippians 2:8).

Jesus was a man—but *don't ever forget He was and is God.*

Centuries before He came, Isaiah had predicted that a child would be born, a Son would be given, with these magnificent names:

Wonderful Counselor, Mighty God,
Everlasting Father, Prince of Peace (Isaiah 9:6).

After His return to heaven, superstitions sprouted about just what His nature really was. And Colossians was written to say, "Look, people, get it straight: Jesus Christ isn't a maxi-angel, He isn't a mini-God—"

---

[1] *The Faces of Jesus,* p. 23.

He is the image of the invisible God, the firstborn over all creation. For by him all things were created . . . by him and for him. He is before all things, and in him all things hold together. . . .

God was pleased to have all his fullness dwell in him (Colossians 1: 15–19)!

In Zechariah 13:6–7, God the Father calls the Messiah His "Associate," His Fellow, His Equal.

In Isaiah 40:10 Christ is called "Jehovah," a name so glorious the Hebrews left out its vowels—"YHWH," making it unpronounceable. And whenever a scribe copying Scriptures wrote out that name, he would first wipe his pen and dip it in fresh ink.

This is our Holy One, Jesus Christ the Lord, the Son of God.

When Peter called Him this—"the Christ, the Son of the living God"—Jesus answered, "Blessed are you" (Matthew 16:16–17).

John told all his readers it was the reason he wrote his book:

That you may believe that Jesus is the Christ, the Son of God, and that by believing you may have life in his name (John 20:31).

Is your heart right now bowed in acknowledgment?
Fix your eyes on Jesus.

A prayer:

Lord, I say with Job,
　"My ears had heard of you
　but now my eyes have seen you" (Job 42:5).
And I say with Thomas,
　"My Lord and my God!" (John 20:28).

The night was long, and the shadows spread
As far as the eye could see;
I stretched my hands to a human Christ,
And He walked through the dark with me!

Out of the dimness at last we came,
Our feet on the dawn-warmed sod;
And I saw by the light of His wondrous eyes
I walked with the Son of God.
—Harriet Ward Beecher

29

Fix your eyes on Jesus the Messiah

If you are Jewish, read these words with care.

(In a sense, we Gentiles are jealous of you!—you're so privileged as God's chosen race. And Jesus should be very special to you, very precious: Racially, He is one of you, not us.)

"Messiah" means "the Anointed One," and your Jewish Scriptures, our Old Testament, said that the Messiah to come would be anointed prophet, priest, and king—all three.

1. Fix your eyes on Jesus, chosen and anointed to be prophet.
The first prophet, Moses, predicted the even greater Prophet to come. Said the Lord God to Moses,

> I will raise up for [the Jews] a prophet like you from among their brothers; I will put my words in his mouth, and he will tell them everything I command him.
>
> If anyone does not listen to my words that the prophet speaks in my name, I myself will call him to account (Deuteronomy 18:18–19).

A prophet is one who comes to speak for God. Jesus was in a sense a double Prophet: He came to *be* God's Word, and He came to *say* God's Word.

> In the beginning was the Word, and the Word was with God, and the Word was God. . . .
> The Word became flesh and lived for a while among us (John 1:1, 14).

And He said,

> The words that I say to you are not my own. Rather it is the Father, living in me, who is doing his work (John 14:10).

Jesus came to fulfill, once and for all, God's great succession of prophets.

2. Fix your eyes on Jesus, chosen and anointed to be priest.
In a sense He was a double Priest: He came to be both the offerer of the sacrifice and the sacrifice itself.
Says Hebrews 2:16–17,

> Made like his brothers in every way . . . [Jesus] became a merciful and faithful high priest in service to God . . . that he might make atonement for the sins of the people.

But Daniel had prophesied,

> The Anointed One will be cut off (Daniel 9:26).

And Isaiah wrote,

> He was cut off from the land of the living;
>   for the transgression of my people he was
>   stricken. . . .
> The Lord makes his life a guilt offering (Isaiah 53:8, 10).

Now, praise the Lord, both you Jews and we Gentiles can be

. . . justified freely by [God's] grace through the redemption that came by Christ Jesus. God presented him as a sacrifice of atonement, through faith in his blood (Romans 3:24–25).

Behold the Lamb of God [announced John, pointing Him out] who takes away the sin of the world (John 1:29).

Jesus came to fulfill, once and for all, God's great system of priest and sacrifice.

3. Fix your eyes on Jesus, chosen and anointed to be king.
Prophet, Priest, King—in one Anointed One, all three come together.
He's the Prophet who brings God to us.
He's the Priest who brings us to God.
And, predicted Zechariah,

It is he who will build the temple of the Lord, and he will be clothed with majesty and will sit and rule on his throne.
And he will be a priest on his throne. And there will be harmony between the two (Zechariah 6:13,—or "between the two offices," translates the Berkeley Version).

A kingly Priest! A priestly King!
And He will be in a sense a double King: not only a great Monarch but a great Servant—both! A Servant King! He defies any similarity to any king before or after. No wonder

The kings of the earth take their stand
        and the rulers gather together
against the Lord
        and against his Anointed One (Psalm 2:2).

This King upsets all their images of how a king should be.

Yet what a stir He's caused—in the Gentile world, as well!
When He was born, Gentile intellectuals traveled from the east inquiring, "Where is the one who has been born King of the Jews?" (Matthew 2:2).

When He was tried, a Gentile political ruler interrogated Him,

> "Are you the King of the Jews?"
> "Yes, it is as you say," Jesus replied (Luke 23:3).

And when He was crucified, for all races to see

> There was a written notice above him, which read,
> "THIS IS THE KING OF THE JEWS" (Luke 23:38).

How could so many Jews miss it? Even as recently before this as 100 B.C., the old prophets were being read with a revival of new hope for the Messiah's soon coming.

But so many predictions spoke of His suffering, and so many others of His reigning—they wondered how both could be right. Some rabbis thought there might be two messiahs: one to suffer, one to reign. Most thought the sufferings applied to the Jews, the glory to the messiah. It was confusing.

Apparently not many thought of one messiah with two comings!

At Jesus' trial it was not to Gentiles but to His own, the Jews, that He explained Himself, and in the context of His larger life. In front of them all—chief priests, teachers, and the full Sanhedrin—

> The high priest said to him, "I charge you under oath by the living God: Tell us if you are the Messiah, the Son of God."
> "Yes, it is as you say," Jesus replied. "But I say to all of you: In the future you will see the Son of Man sitting at the right hand of the Mighty One and coming in the clouds of heaven" (Matthew 26:63–64).

You see, *your King did first business first: He came to redeem before He will come back to reign.* Oh, how we all needed that! He came first to wash us of our sin and make us acceptable in His kingdom.

And we non-Jews were invited to be included! Isaiah had said the Messiah would also be "a light for the Gentiles" (Isaiah 42:6). Millions of us have humbly responded.

Jesus was anointed by God to be "born King of the Jews," but at His first coming He was "cut off." Nevertheless, God makes even the wrath of man ultimately to praise Him (Psalm 76:10), and His cutting off effected salvation for us all—Jew and Gentile alike. Wonderful!

But "I will come again," He said (John 14:3). And at His return, God the Father will indeed "install [his] King on Zion" (Psalm 2:6) to rule gloriously!

Think of it: He'll be a King who reigns with scars in His hands. *What a Savior for you and me!*

His suffering was part of His messiahship—part of what He was anointed to do. Isaiah wrote that He would be "stricken, smitten, afflicted"—words normally used to describe lepers!

And yet Isaiah also wrote,

> He will reign on David's throne
> and over his kingdom,
> establishing and upholding it
> with justice and righteousness
> from that time on and forever.
> The zeal of the Lord Almighty
> will accomplish this (Isaiah 9:7).

And in the New Testament we read that

> God [will exalt] him to the highest place
> and [give] him a name that is above every name,
> that at the name of Jesus every knee should bow . . .
> and every tongue confess that Jesus Christ is Lord,
> to the glory of God the Father (Philippians 2:9–11).

You personally need Him as your Prophet, "to proclaim the year of the Lord's favor" (Isaiah 61:2, Luke 4:18)—*to you!* You can't understand it all without Him.

You need Him as your Priest, bringing you to God, to atone for you and cleanse and forgive you (Psalm 110:4; Hebrews 10:17, 21, 24).

You need Him as your King, to govern your personal life with wisdom and righteousness (Micah 5:2).

*Jewish friend, **fix your eyes on Jesus!***

Why don't you pray to Him this prayer:

God of Abraham, Isaac and Jacob and my God, I receive Your Anointed One Jesus as my Prophet, my Priest, my King—and more: as my Savior, which is what His name "Jesus" means.

I love Him for being all this—even for me.

O Lord, I know that many of my beloved Jewish kinsmen are blind to Him, even as Isaiah prophesied they would be (Isaiah 6:10). But in mercy You have opened my eyes, and *I fix them on Jesus*, and I find my completion in Him.

Thank You, Abba Father!

In the name of Jesus, my Messiah and Savior, amen.

30

Fix your eyes on Jesus crucified

If you've ever been the victim of an action that's blatantly unfair, consider Jesus. Acquitted by the highest court of the land ("I find no basis for a charge against him," John 19:4, 6), He is led away and roughly nailed to a cross to die anyway!

Even in this crisis, the habit of His life continues: He prays. "Father, forgive them. . . ."

Who is "them"?

Not just the Italian soldiers carrying out the act.

Not just the Jewish mob shouting, "Let His blood be on us and on our children!"

Father, forgive all people from Adam on: "all have sinned." All are responsible for His death.

Forgive *me*, Anne Ortlund.

Forgive *you*, reader.

"*. . . For they do not know what they are doing.*"

You didn't know; I didn't know—we weren't even born yet!

Remember the Old Testament Israelites who qualified to live in one of the Cities of Refuge because they'd accidentally killed somebody? We're like that. We crucified Jesus "accidentally and without malice aforethought" (Joshua 20:5).

Nevertheless, we did it: We killed Him. We sinned—and to pay for us, He had to die.

Wrote Johann Heerman in about 1630—and he was right—

Who was the guilty? Who brought this upon Thee?
Alas, my treason, Jesus, hath undone Thee!
'Twas I, Lord Jesus, I it was denied Thee:
I crucified Thee.

And it was so terrible, when it happened all nature went bonkers.
From high noon to mid afternoon, a thick blanket of darkness covered everything.

An earthquake rattled the land so violently that rocks split.

Tombs broke open, and people long dead got up and walked out of their graves and into the city!

The walls of the temple were left undamaged—and yet inside, the great thirty-by-sixty-foot curtain separating the Holy Place (where humans could go) from the Most Holy Place (where dwelt the presence of God) was split right down the middle—interestingly, from the top to the bottom.

"Surely this man was the Son of God!" said one soldier (Mark 15:9). There was no other explanation. And yet—

The scandal of the incarnation . . . [is] the shame of a God Who has so wallowed in the muck and misery of the world that He has become indistinguishable from it.[1]

When we shall see him, there is no beauty that we should desire him. He is despised and rejected of men, a man of sorrows, and acquainted with grief, and we hid as it were our faces from him; he was despised, and we esteemed him not (Isaiah 53:2–3, KJV).

---

[1] Fredrick Buecker, *The Faces of Jesus*, p. 172.

By Thy sweat bloody and clotted! Thy soul in agony,
Thy head crowned with thorns, bruised with staves,
Thine eyes a fountain of tears,
Thine ears full of insults,
Thy mouth moistened with vinegar and gall,
Thy face stained with spitting,
Thy neck bowed down with the burden of the Cross,
Thy back ploughed with the wheals and wounds of the scourge,
Thy pierced hands and feet,
Thy strong cry, Eli, Eli,
Thy heart pierced with the spear,
The water and blood thence flowing,
Thy body broken, Thy blood poured out—
Lord forgive the iniquity of Thy servant
And cover all his sin.[2]

The Lancelot Andrewes quotation above was to end this chapter. But when I'd written these words I got down on my face on the floor.

I groaned, "O God, O God! Have I written this chapter hoping I've written 'powerfully' to touch people about Your crucifixion—so they'd buy the book and I'd make money? Am I standing near the cross hawking my wares to take advantage of the Great Event?"

"Then I'm another Demetrius!" (You remember him, the silversmith. He lived under the shadow of the great goddess idol Artemis, and he didn't want Christ preached because he made a good income selling little silver shrines to the tourists who came to worship her.)

Oh, a thousand, thousand curses on all Demetriuses!

I, too, bow myself at Jesus' cross, in humility and shame. I repent of all my personal sin that put Him there.

You do the same.

O Lord, Lord! Forgive us our dry eyes.

---

[2] Lancelot Andrewes. Quoted by Oswald Sanders, *Christ Incomparable*, p. 141.

31

Fix your eyes on Jesus risen

Jesus' resurrection makes all the difference in your personal life. That's where everything changes!

1. Because of His resurrection He offers you His presence.
In His earthly body Jesus could only be in one place at one time (Luke 10:1). But in His resurrection body—

> On the evening of that first day of the week, when the disciples were together with the doors locked for fear of the Jews, Jesus came and stood among them (John 20:19)

When I'm finished speaking somewhere I can easily worry, "Did I come across too bossy? Did I come across too unfeeling and hard-nosed? Did I put anybody down? Did I offend? Did I intimidate? Did I act like the big know-it-all?" and so on, and so on—and I agonize. *My eyes are on myself.*

But because our Jesus is risen and omnipresent, I can say, "Refocus my eyes on You, Lord. I committed this all to You before I began. I believe You took charge, and that You covered all my humanness that would have distracted from You." And I put that session in my two hands and surrender it to Him again.

And *He is near* (Philippians 4:5), and He comforts me.

At His birth He was given two names, "Jesus" (Matthew 1:21) and "Immanuel" (Matthew 1:22–23). "Jesus" means "Savior," and He was called that all His earthly life.

But "Immanuel" means "God with us," and it's more appropriate now than ever. Standing on the mountain in His resurrection body, ready to go back to heaven, Jesus said something He'd never said before: "I will be with you always" (Matthew 28:20).

He is with you right now, as you read this. **Fix your eyes on Him.**

> The light of Christ surrounds you.
> The love of Christ enfolds you.
> The power of Christ protects you.
> The presence of Christ watches over you.
>   Wherever you are, Christ is.

2. *Because of His resurrection He offers you His peace.* Said the newly risen Christ, "Peace be with you!" (John 20:19–20).

Shalom, the Hebrew word for it, means wholeness, health, well-being, not only outside but inside. *Christ is here, it's okay. In the midst of your problems, it's okay. Peace.*

And when Jesus said *"Shalom"*—or *"salaam"*—He wasn't just saying, "Hi, have a nice day"—*He was bestowing His peace.*

Will you believe that? Will you discipline your heart to take what He offers?

> Thou wilt keep him in perfect peace, whose mind is stayed on thee (Isaiah 26:3, KJV—or "whose eyes are fixed on You"!).

> Now may the Lord of peace himself give you peace
> at all times and in every way (2 Thessalonians 3:16).

3. Because of His resurrection He offers you His purpose.
One of the first things He said in His resurrection body was
this:

> As the Father has sent me, I am sending you (John 20:21).

A brand new principle was suddenly at work!
Back in His earthly life He'd often say, "Now, don't tell
anyone about Me" (Mark 1:34, 43; 3:12; 5:43; 7:36; 8:30; and so
on). From our side of the resurrection, that seems absolutely
strange.
*But when Christ exploded out of that grave, all His followers
exploded into action.* "Go!" He said. "Tell! Be My witnesses to the
ends of the earth!" (Matthew 28:19; Acts 1:8).
The resurrection not only changed *Him,* it changed *them.*
Boy, did they go! Apparently only one of the Twelve died in
their homeland. They went everywhere, "and preached the word
wherever they went" (Acts 8:4). Acts is the book of action.
His new purpose was now their new purpose.
His new life was their new life.
They were now in Him, and He was now in them.
Jesus' resurrection—it meant everything! He's risen; He's alive!
Fix your eyes on Him: What's He telling you to do?
Go for it.

4. Because of His resurrection He offers you His power.
I can't tell you how the fact of Jesus Christ's power en-
courages me and motivates me. When I speak or write, there's
no strength in me to do it on my own.
How could there be?—Hey, when I interact with my children or go on a date with Ray, there's no strength in me to do it
on my own! I'd bungle into arguing or getting critical of someone, or I might be just dull and boring. In myself, I wouldn't
have the words to bless or lift or even be fun.

Let me give you here a very important truth for your living:

Your weaknesses—totally acknowledged and continually real-ized—give you your only claim and access to His resurrection power.

I've been a Christian since I was about six years old, and I don't think I'm any stronger now than when I was six. And it's all right with me.

Are you weak? The Lord doesn't take that weakness away. He says, "My power is made perfect in weakness" (2 Corinthians 12:9).

And Paul's response to this was,

> Therefore I will boast all the more gladly about my weaknesses, so that Christ's power may rest upon me. . . .
> When I am weak, then I am strong (2 Corinthians 12:9–10).

Don't be concerned or embarrassed over your weaknesses. Don't try to forget them or hide them or pray to conquer them or be freed from them.

Jesus doesn't *make you stronger*. The risen Lord said, "You will receive power when the Holy Spirit comes upon you" (Acts 1:8). It's His power only; it always has been, always will be. He doesn't lessen your weaknesses and add a little of His strength, the way I blend a glass of iced tea.

Your total weakness and His total strength are to coexist side by side.

> We have this treasure in jars of clay, to show that this all-surpassing power is from God and not from us (2 Corinthians 4:7).

In all your struggles and temptations, *fix your eyes on the resurrected Jesus!*

Let the only measure of your expectations
for yourself
be the power of Jesus Christ

Then you can live a truly powerful life—not because you're no longer weak, but because, being weak, you count on His power to work in you.

We had company for dinner the other night, and the two lamps flanking the couch wouldn't go on. Oh, well. . . . But after our friends had left, Ray investigated and found the plug in the wall socket was sort of sagging out and had lost its connection.

Never mind your weaknesses; just make sure you're solidly connected, strongly "abiding in Him."

Then *expect the power of His resurrection to work in your life.*

> With that he breathed on them and said, "Receive the Holy Spirit." (John 20:22).

Right now, sit loose in your chair.

Breathe out—I'm doing it, too—as if expelling your lack of confidence in His abilities on your behalf.

Now prayerfully breathe in, in a sense, a fresh filling of His Holy Spirit. Breathe in new expectations of His victories in your life.

Fix your eyes on Jesus.

Prayer:

O wonderful Lord Jesus Christ of the empty tomb,
I receive anew Your presence.
I receive anew Your peace.
I receive anew Your purpose.
I receive anew Your power.
> In Your own dear name, amen.

"Look to the Lord and his strength" (Psalm 105:4).

Looking at Jesus will infuse your life with power.

Looking much at Jesus will infuse your life with much power.

Looking continually at Jesus will infuse your life with continual power.

32

Fix your eyes on Jesus
the Eternal One

The "Ancient of Days," Daniel called Him.

Take a long, hard look at Jesus Christ in the far-away past . . .
back, back, back. . . .

Back before creation, the Father had loved Him (John 17:24).

Back before the world began, He shared the Father's glory
(John 17:5), and with Him made all things (Colossians 1:16).

He declares, speaking as our Wisdom (1 Corinthians 1:30),

I was there when he set the heavens in place . . .
     and when he marked out the foundation of the earth.
Then was I the craftsman at his side (Proverbs 8:27, 29, 30).

God in Christ separated light from darkness,
     separated water above from water below,
          separated seas from dry ground.

God in Christ ordered the ground to fill up with seeds producing vegetation,
> the waters to fill up with fish,
>> the land to fill up with animals and insects. . . .

Then *God in Christ* commanded the plants and creatures to die,
> their bodies to fall back into the ground,
>> their remains to compress and become coal, diamonds, oil, gas—vast, vast reserves of materiel, probably not all discovered even yet. . . .

Why?

All these lived not for themselves but for us. God in Christ was forming them long ago to heat winters they would never live through, to light buildings they would never see.

God in Christ, with infinite wisdom and skill and love, was preparing a place for us. (The Ancient of Days, the Eternal One, loved us even back then.)

Yet we've been destroying the place He prepared, by our sin.

How sad God must have been, to have to tell Adam, "Because you listened to your wife and ate . . . cursed is the ground" (Genesis 3:17)!

And ever since then,

> We know that the whole creation has been groaning as in the pains of childbirth right up to the present time (Romans 8: 22).

The earth dries up and withers. . . .
The earth is defiled by its people;
> they have disobeyed the laws . . .
therefore a curse consumes the earth (Isaiah 24:4–6).

A woman once exclaimed to her famous pastor, Dr. Charles Spurgeon, "Oh, Dr. Spurgeon, I'm afraid the world is coming to an end!"

"Never mind, my dear," he said; "we can get along without it."

That's the good news!

Fix your eyes on Jesus! He knew all along what we would do with the wonderful place He gave us, His gift prepared with such love and skill—and He's getting a replacement ready:

> Do not let your hearts be troubled. . . . In my Father's house are many rooms. . . . I am going there to prepare a place for you (John 14:1–2)

—a *second place for us in our resurrection, perfection, glory!*

If this first place was so beautiful and so equipped, what will the new one be like? Jesus hasn't forgotten you; He has you in His heart. He's been getting another place ready, and He says, "I am making everything new!" (Revelation 5:13).

Fix your eyes on Jesus, and you'll stumble on wonder after wonder—and every wonder will be true.

Now take a long, hard look at Jesus in the future. Then every creature will be singing,

> To him who sits on the throne and to the Lamb
> be praise and honor and glory and power,
>   for ever and ever! (Revelation 5:13).

Surely you'll want to bow your knees to pray to such a One:

> Lord, I'm "lost in wonder, love, and praise."
> Lord, You have told me that You know the plans You have for me, plans to prosper me and not to harm me, plans to give me hope and a future (Jeremiah 29:11).
> I can hardly wait.
> Lord, I look at Your eternal past and I see it marred by our sin. But I look at Your eternal future—and my eternal future with You—and my heart leaps.
> Even so, come, Lord Jesus.
> Amen and amen.

Thou great I AM,
Fill my mind with elevation and grandeur
    at the thought of a Being
   with whom one day is as a thousand years,
      and a thousand years as one day,
A mighty God who, amidst the lapse of worlds,
   and the revolutions of empires,
   feels no variableness,
   but is glorious in immortality.
May I rejoice that, while men die, the Lord lives;
   that, while all creatures are broken reeds,
           empty cisterns,
           fading flowers,
           withering grass,
   he is the rock of ages,
     the fountain of living waters.
        —Old Puritan prayer

33

Fix your eyes on Jesus coming again

At that electrifying point in time, nobody will have to be told any more; *every eye in the universe will be fixed on Jesus.* Says Revelation 1:7,

> Look, he is coming with the clouds,
>   and every eye will see him,
> even those who pierced him;
>   and all peoples of the earth will mourn because of him.

What a shock! At that moment millions will be begging, *"Wait!* Wait, I'm not ready!"

But *time will have stopped.*
And the Spirit will never again plead, "Today, if you hear his voice, do not harden your hearts" (Hebrews 4:7)—
There'll be no more "today"!

Suddenly every person will be caught in his tracks. Like action on television, in an instant the frame will freeze! And then this verse will come true:

Let him who does wrong continue to do wrong;
Let him who is vile continue to be vile;
Let him who does right continue to do right,
And let him who is holy continue to be holy (Revelation 22:11).

And it will be judgment time.

I was carelessly tootling along in the car the other day doing sixty-five in a fifty-five-mile-an-hour zone, and not even conscience-stricken because all the cars around me were going at least that fast.

But suddenly at the side of the road was a brand new gadget our City of Newport Beach had just installed: It recorded *my personal speed*—only mine—in huge numbers for all the world to see. Newport Beach with all its powers of authority and punishment was scrutinizing *me*—at that moment only lil' ol' me. I tell you, I felt as guilty as sin. My heart raced as I slowed down to fifty-five and looked in my mirror for the Long Arm of the Law. There wasn't any. Whew.

But that was nothing compared with the moment when the Lord Jesus as Judge will fix His eye on me.

For we must all appear before the judgment seat of Christ, that each one may receive what is due him for the things done in the body, whether good or bad (2 Corinthians 5:10).

That's why 1 John 2:28 says,

Dear children, *continue* [or abide] *in him,* so that when he appears, we may be confident and unashamed before him at his coming.

Just the same, consider these wonderful facts:

1. He loves us! (1 John 3:1).
2. We're going to be like Him! (1 John 3:2).

When at His return He wants to so gloriously transform you— don't, don't you dare take advantage of that promise and fool around now. You'd be so embarrassed, so full of regrets!

Everyone who has this hope in him *purifies himself* (1 John 3:3).

Let's pray together:

O Lord God, we have all eternity to enjoy our rewards, as Amy Carmichael said, and only a few short years to win them.

Lord, *write eternity on my eyeballs.* May I see all things from Your perspective—and most of all, may I see You Yourself.

O Lord, I want to live at this moment,
      and the rest of this day,
         and the rest of my life,
so that I can continually say, "Come, Lord Jesus! Come soon! Come now!"

Fix my eyes on You.

In Your precious name, amen.

Lord of the cloud and fire,
I am a stranger, with a stranger's indifference;
My hands hold a pilgrim's staff,
My march is Zionward,
My eyes are toward the coming of the Lord.
                          —Old Puritan prayer

PART 4

Fix your eyes on Jesus
to get focus

34

Fix your eyes on Jesus
and on nothing else clearly

As you're reading this book page right now, your eyes are focused only on the print. You're somewhat aware of your arms,

     your lap,

     your chair,

     your surroundings

—aware enough that you wouldn't suddenly move so that you'd bump against something; aware enough that you'd know if some dog, for instance, or a person suddenly arrived on the scene that you needed to know about. So although your peripheral vision is a safeguard, a buffer zone, it doesn't occupy your immediate attention.

Live your life something like that. When you fix your eyes on Jesus your focus will be on Him, but your peripheral vision will be enough to take care of the rest.

Hebrews 12:2 is our verse: "Fix your eyes on Jesus." But there's a meaning in the original words that's lost in most translations: it indicates looking *away* to Jesus—with such concentration that you don't see anything else quite as clearly.

"Away": that's the untranslated adverb.

I was going to be traveling to Texas on "book business." It had been a while since I'd had time to think about my wardrobe, and last week, deep in ministry, God brought it to my mind.

(You may not be in "full-time ministry," as we use that phrase, but bear with my illustration anyway.)

Around the edges of my consciousness He planted the thought, "You need a couple of dresses for Texas and for summer church and conference speaking."

A day or two later I was sitting in a restaurant engrossed in eating lunch, reading my Bible and writing my prayers. Afterward as I turned to go I realized that next door was women's clothing. I remembered my need, and there in plain view were two simple summer dresses: my size, my price, my autumn colors. On the spot I got them, with shoes for one and earrings for the other, and I knew that what I already had at home would finish the two outfits. Thank You, Abba Father. . . .

It will probably be a year before I need to get any further summer clothes.

Now, sometimes my life isn't that smooth and efficient. Sometimes God deliberately builds hassle into my life; He knows when I need it to grow. He's so kind!

But as a general rule for living, Matthew 6:33 will always be true: "Seek first his kingdom and his righteousness, and dresses, shoes, and earrings will be given to you as well."

—Oh, no, that's not quite how the verse goes: "all these things"—whatever is needed to help you live while you "seek first."

The point is, *look away to Jesus.*

Let's pray about this:

Heavenly Father, may the focus of my life be—
        Not on myself (page 173)
        Not on others (page 175)
        Not on my troubles (page 180)
        Not on material things (page 183)
        Not on the devil (page 186)
        Not on my sins (page 192)
        Not on false hopes (page 201)
        Not on ugliness (page 205)

Help me to look away from all these to Jesus!
In His worthy name, amen.

Oh, fix our earnest gaze
So wholly, Lord, on You,
That with Your beauty occupied
All else is dimmer view.

35

Fix your eyes on Jesus
and not on yourself

You get no forgiveness from just looking at all your sins.

You get no healing, just concentrating on your diseases.

You get no redemption, just studying the pit you're in.

You get no crowning with glory, just fixing your eyes on your failures.

You get no fulfillment of desires, just looking at all you don't have.

You get no renewal from focusing on your oldness, staleness, dryness.

Only He
   "forgives all [your] sins . . .
   heals all [your] diseases . . .
   redeems [your] life from the pit . . .
   crowns [you] with love and compassion . . .
   satisfies [your] desires with good things,

so that [your] youth is renewed like the eagle's"
(Psalm 103:3–5).

Only He!
Look to yourself, and ultimately you'll be embarrassed. But

Those who look to him are radiant;
    their faces are never covered with shame (Psalm 34:5).

Let's pray:

Lord, I'm ready to be radiant.
You know my battle! You know how often my attention is on myself. Then I'm shut up, as Malcolm Muggeridge says, in the dark prison of my own ego.

Lord Jesus, I fix my eyes on You.
I come out into radiant sunshine; I'm walking in the light! But may my joy not be in the light as much as in You.
For Your own dear sake, amen.

36

Fix your eyes on Jesus
and not on others

Let me tell you how this truth recently hit home to me.

Sometimes Ray and I—and so do you—see generations slip. You see

> a husband and wife going hard after the Lord;
> their children attending church more often than not;
> and their grandchildren totally uninterested in
> spiritual things.

And through the years we've prayed, "Lord, *keep the fire hot!* Keep our children fervent for You, our grandchildren fervent for You, our great grandchildren. . . ." And God, out of His amazing grace and not because we're deserving, has been answering our prayers.

So you can understand our thrill when the first grandchild, Lisa, so zealous for God, became engaged to wonderful Mark, who loves Him as much as she does.

I tell you what I've said so far with much prayer, saying, "Lord, don't let this be bragging! So many godly parents have rebellious children, and we're no better."

But I tell you the next part of the story with even more prayer, knowing I'm opening myself up for attack.

Help me, Jesus.

By the night of the wedding I was giddy with joy. God was so faithful to hear our prayers; Lisa and Mark were such treasures. Pastors Ray and John, grandfather and father of the bride, performed the ceremony before all John's loving congregation. . . .

("... Who gives this woman to be married to this man?"

"Your daughter and I do. . . ." We choked with laughter and tears. . . .)

At the reception (filled with the Spirit but no "spirits"), the little band began a happy beat, and Ray and I were too exhilarated to sit still any longer. We don't know how to dance, but we were silly enough that night to discover we could *wiggle without touching* with the best of them. I hoofed around with Ray, with son Nels, and with a teenage Iranian boy our grandson had just led to know Christ.

(Some readers are reacting, "Yea for the grandson! Yea for the new believer!" And some are reacting, "Boo for corrupting a new Christian!" Help me, Lord.)

Neither Nels nor the new friend knew any more about dancing than we did, but it was celebration time, and we were all full of it. "I could have danced (?) all night. . . ."

But at a break a girl came up to me and said, "I'm from northern California, and my small group and I have been so blessed studying your book *Discipling One Another*. May I take your picture?"

Suddenly I came to—and I thought, "Dear Lord, what has she been watching? I wouldn't for the world offend another Christian."

I thought of Romans 14 and the need to live conservatively for others' sakes.

. . . Then I thought, "The bride's *grandmother?* Gimme a break."

. . . Then I thought of David's uninhibited happiness in 2 Samuel 6, and, like him, I said to myself, "It was before the Lord. . . ."

In telling you this, reader, I'm exposed and vulnerable, and I'm humbly asking God to cover me from criticisms, for His sake. I tell it to you not to "justify dancing"—horrors, no—but because I learned again on Lisa's wedding night that in*terior motives, not exterior actions, are the bottom line.*

> The Lord does not look at the things man looks at.
> Man looks at the outward appearance, but the Lord looks
> at the heart (1 Samuel 16:7).

When He sees a rebellious heart, even that man's *plowing* is sin (Proverbs 21:4); he can't do *anything* right.

But this whole issue of "what's right? what's wrong?" is the reason for Romans 14, and the point of it is,
Fix your eyes not on others but on Jesus.

Never mind what other Christians do or don't do; "to his own master [not to you or me] he stands or falls" (v. 4). "Therefore let us stop passing judgment on one another" (v. 13).

"Whatever we do, let's do it *to the Lord*," says Romans 14. "And whatever we decide *not* to do, let's abstain *to the Lord*."

All eyes directed up!

It's a dumb kind of Christianity that constantly looks sideways to check out what each other is doing. It will make us clean the outside of the cup while inside we may be full of wickedness (Luke 11:39): deceit, criticisms, and outward show.

Don't fix your eyes on others—
Fix your eyes on Jesus, and give Him pleasure.

Let's pray to Him:

How different Your flowers are, O blessed Creator,
how different Your insects,
how different Your sea creatures,
how different Your children!
    O Spirit of God, clothe me with compassion, kindness,
humility, gentleness, and patience. May I bear with others,
forgive others, truly love others. . . .

    And *most of all, fix my eyes on Jesus!*
In His own name, amen.

Guy King says that there's a gold running cup on another man's mantel that could have been—should have been—on his own.

He was running toward the tape, coming in number one.

Somebody was trailing on his right, and he shot a look to see where he was. It was the split-second distraction that his competitor needed, and he flashed by him and won.

"Our sole safety [as Christians]," says Guy King, "is to be found in keeping our eyes averted . . . from others, and keeping them unswervingly 'looking unto Jesus.'"

—Brought In, pp. 72–73

37

Fix your eyes on Jesus and not on your troubles

I look to Thee in every need
  And never look in vain;
I feel Thy strong and tender love
  And all is well again:
The thought of Thee is mightier far
  Than sin and pain and sorrow are.
          —*Samuel Longfellow*

"Sin and pain and sorrow"—all your troubles—are so limited and weak, they're not worthy of your full concentration.

Your troubles can't shut off the power of God's Spirit to work on your behalf.

They can't change His long-range plans for you.

They can't thwart the ability of His Word to comfort and direct you.

They can't lessen the availability of your Christian brothers and sisters to encourage you.

They can't reduce your eternal life!

Then don't let them overcome you.

Fix your eyes on Jesus, and ask Him for godly optimism, steadiness, endurance.

Take courage from Psalm 25:15:

My eyes are ever on the Lord,
    for only he will release my feet from the snare.

Offer to Him this prayer:

Dear Lord God, thank You for giving me my troubles! First Peter 1:7 says that You've given them to prove that my faith is genuine, when it gets refined in these fires; and that they will result in praise, glory, and honor to You.

Then, Lord, I don't fix my eyes on my troubles but on You. I offer You my praise, glory and honor! I'm so happy that these very trials are proving that my faith is in You and I trust You.

Alleluia!

In Christ's dear name, amen.

For every one look at your problems,
your weaknesses, your failures—
take ten looks at Jesus.

—Robert Murray McCheyne,
fiery Scottish preacher
who died at the age
of twenty-nine

38

Fix your eyes on Jesus
and not on material things

Here's a nineteenth-century person riding along in his carriage on a dark but star-lit night, says Søren Kierkegaard, as paraphrased by Anne Ortlund.

He's got all his coach lights on, so as he drives along he can see in front of him just fine. But with those strong lights all around him he can't see the stars very well—just the way if you're a materialist you can't see Jesus very well.

Now, says Kierkegaard, on this dark but star-lit night here comes a poor peasant. He has no carriage and no lights at all, so you'd think he'd get a glorious view of the stars. The only problem is, he's probably so busy looking down to make sure he doesn't fall in a hole, he doesn't see the stars, either.

And if you get rid of every single material possession—just the business of living would certainly be more awkward, and probably be so distracting and consuming that you wouldn't fix your eyes on Jesus, either. Asceticism is no answer.

So the big question is: How many lanterns do you need? How many material things are just the right amount, to live efficiently enough and yet still have a good sight of Jesus?

The "good life" isn't achieved by gross consumption of material goods. (Do you know that the word "miser," one who hoards, and the word "misery" come from exactly the same root?)

But neither is "the good life" achieved by *the least possible* consumption of material goods.

Says Vernard Eller,

> The point is that these things can be good—very good—*if they are used to support man's relationship to God rather than compete with it.*[1]

As I write these words I'm shut off from the phone and all activities, in the total quiet of a kind friend's beach condo, his "second home." At this moment it's a lantern to light my way to see how to write this book. My friend is using his condo not to "compete with God" but to "support man's relationship to Him." And I know his heart as well as I know my own—that we both want to keep our lives dark enough to see the stars.

Nobody can tell you how many lanterns you personally need, and don't judge anyone else's decisions. The only point is, keep your own lanterns few enough so that most of all, you can see Him!

> Turn your eyes upon Jesus,
>   Look full in His wonderful face,
> And the things of earth will grow strangely dim,
>   In the light of His glory and grace.[2]

---

[1] *The Simple Life,* pp. 28–29.

[2] Copyright 1922. Renewal 1950 by H. H. Lemmel. Assigned to Singspiration, Inc.

Prayer songs. Sing the hymn quoted above, and then, if you know it, sing to Him this one:

> Open my eyes, Lord; I want to see Jesus,
>> To reach out and touch Him and say that I love Him.
> Open my ears, Lord; please help me to listen.
>> Open my eyes, Lord; I want to see Jesus![3]

---

[3]Words and music by Bob Cull. Copyright 1976 by Maranatha Music, Box 1396, Costa Mesa, California 92626.

39

Fix your eyes on Jesus
and not on the devil

Spiritual warfare is the latest "game" some Christians are trying to play, for several reasons. Think about it.

There are three major negative influences to blame for all our troubles: the world, the flesh, and the devil.

Many Christians really like the world, these days. They're fascinated by it, they're cozying up to it, they're copying it. So they're saying—perhaps unconsciously—"Let's not blame the world for our problems—we might have to back off from it."

And *many Christians are trying hard to like the flesh.* They think putting it down would damage their self-image. So they're saying—not in actual words—"Let's not blame the flesh—that would be blaming *me.*" ("If I can wriggle out of responsibility and blame all my ills on an external force out there, it takes 'me' off the hook.")

So *let's blame the devil!* I really didn't want to—"the devil made me do it."

Perhaps another reason we play "spiritual warfare" is because it's sensational; teaching about it is exciting; it raises a flap; it's cops and robbers on a universal scale.

An amazing number of Christians these days are full of fear, not full of faith—because their eyes are fixed on the devil, not fixed on Jesus.

When I was about five, a bigger neighbor girl would get hold of me and put me in a dark room and tell me ghost stories. One day she told me about the Red Hands. She said they were out to get me and that I wasn't safe a minute.

I took off.

I walked for miles before Daddy, out scouting in his car, found me and brought me home again.

But for weeks after that, I wouldn't go into a dark room alone; somebody had to precede me and turn on lights first. (This was before switches were by the door.)

And to get into my bed I'd make a mighty leap—so the Red Hands under my bed couldn't grab my ankles. I was a mess.

The difference between the Red Hands and the devil is that *the devil is real.*

> Be self-controlled and alert. Your enemy the devil prowls around like a roaring lion looking for someone to devour (1 Peter 5:8).

Then shouldn't we be constantly terrified, like little Anne Sweet?

C.S. Lewis writes this:

> There are two equal and opposite errors into which our race can fall about the devils. One is to disbelieve in their existence. The other is to believe, and to feel an excessive and unhealthy interest in them.[1]

---

[1] C.S. Lewis, *The Screwtape Letters.*

Don't fix your eyes on the devil. I hear you're never supposed to make eye contact with an unfamiliar, especially an unfriendly, dog; he takes that as a threat.

Well, don't get over-occupied with Satan, either.

Martin Luther once wrote,

> One does not gain much ground against the devil with a lengthy disputation; but with brief words and replies, such as: "I am a Christian, of the same flesh and blood as is my Lord Christ, the Son of God. Settle your accounts with Him."
> Then the devil does not stay long.

I have a better idea. (Who am I to improve on Martin Luther?!) *Don't talk to him at all.* Jude says that fools are those who

> . . . slander celestial beings. But even the archangel Michael, when he was disputing with the devil about the body of Moses, did not dare bring a slanderous accusation against [the devil], but said, "The Lord rebuke you!"
> Yet these men speak abusively against whatever they do not understand (v. 8–10).

The devil is too dangerous, too "un-understood," too powerful for us to stand up and try to eyeball him. I don't know, maybe he thinks it's just plain hilarious when you or I try to "rebuke" him; even the great Michael didn't dare to.

I notice in Zechariah, chapter 3, when the devil was hassling Joshua the high priest—spiritually by far the most important man of that day—that *the Lord Himself rebuked the devil on behalf of Joshua.*

So *when you're in turmoil what do you do?*
First, seek to pin down the primary cause of your situation.

1. Is the world to blame?
Have you been "worldly"—involved with the world, secretly admiring it, copying its thinking, its lifestyle?

> Don't you know that friendship with the world is ha-
> tred toward God? (James 4:4).

> What fellowship can light have with darkness? . . .
> "Therefore come out from them
> and be separate.
> Touch no unclean thing,
> and I will receive you" . . . says the Lord
> Almighty (2 Corinthians 6:14–18).

Repent of your fooling around; extricate yourself! *Fix your
eyes only on Jesus,* and tell Him you want to love only Him.

2. Is the flesh to blame?
Did you make bad choices? Should you yourself take responsibility for your trouble?

> Do not be deceived: God cannot be mocked. A man
> reaps what he sows. The one who sows to please his sinful
> nature [or flesh], from that [flesh] will reap destruction
> (Galatians 6:7–8).

Repent of what you did, or said, or thought, all by yourself. Let God forgive you and cleanse you totally—and then *fix
your eyes on Jesus.*

3. Is the devil to blame?
Ephesians 6 is the classic chapter on what to do about Satan. How do you struggle against "the powers of this dark world
and against the spiritual forces of evil in the heavenly realms"?
This chapter in Ephesians doesn't suggest a quick fix. Let's
look.
First, Ephesians 6's solution is preventitive. You start *now,*
ahead of time:

> Put on the full armor of God, so that when the day of
> evil comes, you may be able to stand your ground, and af-
> ter you have done everything, to stand (Ephesians 6:13).

What, Lord? You mean to say we don't get to start right now whipping our sword around, and maybe like Peter cut off somebody's ear?

No, the Lord Himself will do your fighting for you; He's definitely more qualified. Your place is to *stand*.

Second, Ephesians 6's solution is thorough. "After you have done everything"!

What must you do? "Put on the full armor"—don't miss a single piece—of truth, righteousness, readiness that comes from the gospel, faith, salvation, and the Word of God; and through it all, praying always.

Put on every one of these:

1. *Salvation:* Make sure you're born again.

2. *The Word of God:* Get into a Bible class or a Bible correspondence course or some kind of instruction.

3. *Truth:* Learn right doctrine; expose yourself to Bible preaching, good radio teaching.

4. *Prayer:* It's not easy but crucial: keep a daily quiet time.

5. *Readiness that comes from the gospel:* Know what "the gospel," in a nutshell, really is—it's found, for instance, in 1 Corinthians 15:1–4—so you can share it.

6. *Righteousness:* Be careful to maintain moral integrity.

7. *Faith:* Trust yourself utterly to the Lord.

And notice something else:

Third, Ephesians 6's solution is positive! This armor against the devil is an aggressively happy, good lifestyle.

Simply seek to live a diligent Christian life. That's the unsensational, steady, pleasant, poised, serene stance of power that will make the devil go bother somebody else.

> The prince of darkness grim,
> We tremble not for him!

Fix your eyes on Jesus—and Satan will probably stay far away.

Prayer:

I reject the devil, O Lord. I reject his influence in my life. I ask You to rebuke him and, if it's Your will, keep him far away from me. Lord, I **fix my eyes on Jesus;** I want to live aggressively in His disciplines.

Lord, clothe me with the perfection of your seven pieces of armor:

> With truth,
> With righteousness,
> With the readiness that comes from the gospel,
> With faith,
> With salvation,
> With Your Word,
> And with prayer.

In the strong name of the Lord Jesus Christ, amen.

40

Fix your eyes on Jesus
and not on your sins

"Looking at the sin," wrote Theodore Monod, "only gives death; looking at Jesus gives life."

Psalm 32:3–4 and Psalm 38:3–10 both say that your personal sins, unrelieved by Jesus, can give you
physical weakness,
depression,
heart palpitations,
back pains,
a tendency to infections,
vision problems,
and even bad posture.

Right now are you more aware of your sins than you are of Jesus? Focusing on them will do you in. There's no godliness in continually mourning over your sins. There's no merit in spending your life wringing your hands and crying, "I'm such a sinner! Oh, my awful sins!"

Any occupation with self is, in itself, sin. So don't even make the matter of seeking to *renounce* your sins the big focus of your life.

If you're a man, do you play with toy cars? Probably not. You did as a boy—but there came a time when driving a real one was more fun, and you just quit playing with the others. You didn't give up toy cars; *they gave up you.*

If you're a woman, do you play with dolls? Probably not. You used to—but one day a fellow asked you out, and you discovered something better! You didn't give up dolls; *they gave up you.*

And when you fix your eyes on Jesus and you find out that He's flooding into you His resurrection life and power— you don't renounce a life of sin; *it will renounce you.*

Dr. Donald Grey Barnhouse used to say,

There are two ways of walking from London to Edinburgh. You can walk backwards all the way, looking back at London; or you can turn your back on London and walk with your face toward Edinburgh.

There are two ways in which you can be separated from the world. You can have your back toward Christ and look at the world and say, "I am renouncing the world," or you can look toward the Lord Jesus and say, "Lord, I am coming toward You;" and every step you take toward the Lord you will find yourself further from all the rest of those things.[1]

Fix your eyes on Jesus.

---

[1] *The Keswick Week, 1955,* p. 146.

Prayer:

Lord, You have said that "if we confess our sins, [You are] faithful and just and will forgive us our sins and purify us from all unrighteousness" (1 John 1:9).
Lord, I do that right now.

[Spend some leisurely time confessing to Him, in words, your sins.]

O Lord, I realize how painfully incomplete this list is. You are so pure, I don't even begin to know all the multitude of ways that I offend a holy God.

But, Lord, Your promise is that if I confess what I do know, You will purify me *from all unrighteousness*—everything I don't know as well and make me wholly clean.

How wonderful! Thank You, Father! What a blessing!

And now, my God, I don't want to spend my life walking backwards, with my eyes always fixed on what I'm discarding.

"Forgetting those things that are behind . . . I press on toward the goal" (Philippians 3:13–14).

Lord, what a happy way to walk, with my face toward You! I *fix my eyes on Jesus.*

"The path of the just is like the shining light, that shineth more and more unto the perfect day" (Proverbs 4:18, KJV).

Alleluia!

*Sin will keep you
from fixing your eyes on Jesus,
or
fixing your eyes on Jesus
will keep you
from sin.*

41

Fix your eyes on Jesus
and not on the church

Have you noticed how when you "talk church" to Christians you don't know, you've immediately built a wall between you?

But if you "talk Jesus"—if you fix your eyes on Him—you're united?

The Samaritan woman who talked to Jesus at the well (John 4) fell into the "talk church" trap. Jesus was talking about "living water"—Himself—and she didn't know what to make of it except that it must be related to organized religion.

So she brashly waded in: "Our [Samaritan] fathers worshiped on this mountain, but you Jews claim that the place where we must worship is in Jerusalem."

See how when we "talk church," we put labels on each other and we're immediately divisive?

"You Jews, we Samaritans."

"You're charismatic, we're not."

"You're Lutheran, we're Baptist."

"You worship on Sunday, we worship on Saturday."

"You raise your hands, we never do that."

"You're independent, we're denominational."

"You're formal, we're informal."

"You ordain women, we don't allow that."

And on and on.

No church is good enough to be on a level with Jesus.

No "denominational distinctives" are important enough to overshadow Him.

No cause,

no creed,

no baptism,

no party,

no ministry,

no customs,

no rules,

no doctrine,

no doctrine teacher,

no movement,

no movement leader,

no local pastor,

no vision,

no specialty—

no aspect of Christianity, whatever it is and however good it may be, can be on a par with the firstness of Jesus.

Ray was asked one Sunday to preach at a church in San Diego, not far from where we live. He and Nels and I got the brilliant idea of going for the weekend and incorporating the preaching into a little mini-vacation.

Settled in our motel on Saturday, we bought a newspaper and discovered that Sunday afternoon the San Diego Symphony

Orchestra was going to be giving a free concert on the campus of the University of California at San Diego. It sounded great.

So after Ray preached, we dropped by a cafeteria for some lunch and then headed for the campus. We hauled a blanket out of the trunk of the car, and spread it on the grass in the sunshine—along with thousands of others.

Some had obviously come, as we had, from church; the guys peeled off their coats and ties, and the gals kicked off their heels. . . .

Some had just as obviously come from the beach; they had on their cut-offs and thongs or their bikinis and bare feet. . . . Some got out their beer bottles. . . .

But when the orchestra began playing, nobody thought any more about how each other looked or what each other did. We were all concentrating beyond ourselves; *we were all caught up in the same beauty.*

For Christian unity in the midst of Christian variety,
    fix your eyes on Jesus.

Prayer:

O Lord, we Christians tend to get confused in the midst of diversity! Like Peter on the Mountain of Transfiguration, we start to build three tabernacles, or more.

Father, to make my heart broad, keep my vision narrowed.

Help me to look up and see no one except Jesus (Matthew 17:8).

In His matchless name, amen.

42

Fix your eyes on Jesus
and not on your spiritual gifts

Narcissus, in Greek mythology, pined away to almost nothing for love of his own reflection in water—and so do Christians who catch his disease.

We live in a narcissistic age—even within Christianity. Many of us believers have an excessive interest in—and affection for—

> ourselves,
> our feelings,
> our relationships,
> our abilities,
> our lifestyles,
> our spiritual development,
> our knowledge,
> our growth,
> our maturity—

anything involving *us!* So a few years ago, studying spiritual gifts was a "natural"—complete with personality testings.

(More recently it's been spiritual warfare. Studies like these are good and important in their place, but simply not worthy of such temporary, intense hype.

We're like a bunch of blackbirds sitting on a telephone wire. One flies off to another telephone wire, so everybody flies off and joins him on that one. . . . Then another flies off to another telephone wire, so everybody flies and settles on that one. . . .

When our eyes aren't fixed on Jesus, Ephesians 4:14 says we can be "infants, tossed back and forth by the waves, and blown here and there by every wind of doctrine.")

The Holy Spirit gives spiritual gifts not for ourselves but *for service:*

> Each one should use whatever gift he has received to serve others, faithfully administering God's grace in its various forms (1 Peter 4:10).

Yesterday's grace passed with yesterday's service. Today's grace is only for today. Gifts are bestowed for each situation's need in the body, and they're not given to look at but *to use.*
Says Theodore Monod,

> We are not to gloat over [our gifts] as treasures, counting up our riches, but to spend them immediately and remain poor, "looking unto Jesus."[1]

Let's pray to Him:

> Lord, I wasn't comfortable anyway with all that self-preoccupation. It put me in the arena of competition and coveting.
> *I fix my eyes on You;* and I say, Lord Jesus, however You want to use me to help Your people, I'm available.
> I love You, Lord! In Your blessed name, amen.

---

[1] *Looking unto Jesus*, p. 17.

43

Fix your eyes on Jesus
and not on today's false helps

When you've got a problem, false advice is on all sides of you. And it may sound so beautiful, so wonderful, so religious—even so biblical!

Just take a Bible verse out of context—or what's even more subtle, change its punctuation a little—*and you've got false advice.*

Take this well-known Psalm 121:1, in the Old King James Version:

> I will lift up mine eyes unto the hills,
> from whence cometh my help.

Have you heard that one? It sounds as if you can just fix your eyes on nature and somehow get strength.

No, no! The later versions correct that; they don't have a comma there, they have a period and then a question mark:

> I will lift up mine eyes unto the hills [period].
> From whence cometh my help?

And then it answers its own question:

> My help cometh from the Lord,
> who made heaven and earth.

Do you know what those hills were like in the psalmist's days? Pure treachery.

Shrines to Baal and Asgerah and other pagan gods were built on hilltops, and at those shrines you could buy a false god's "protection." The hills were places of superstition and spells and magic. The people's dangers were real, but those solutions were phony.

False religions and so-called "Christians" who are misled and misleading are all around you, as thick as the Israeli hills. They're mines; they're booby traps.

You can see them on television or hear them on radio.

You can let them walk into your home, or you can walk into their reading rooms.

You can order their literature—which on the surface sounds as if they're in favor of mother and opposed to smog.

You can go into their "churches" to "worship"—the music may be marvelous.

Remember, Satan isn't always ugly; he can also masquerade "as an angel of light. It is not surprising, then, if his servants masquerade as servants of righteousness" (2 Corinthians 11:14–15).

Where will you lift up *your* eyes? Be very careful.

Not to the "hills," the "high places" of Satan.

Your help comes only, only from the Lord.

Go to a Bible-preaching church. Seek out friends who fellowship around Christ. Read His Word and pray.

Fix your eyes only on Jesus.

Let's pray.

O my Father! You know how easily Satan can mislead us! Error, deceit, wickedness is around me on all sides.

You only are my help. Keep me exposed to Your truth, and open my mind to understand it and my heart to receive it.

Fix my eyes steadfastly on Your dear Son, who is the Way, the Truth, and the Life. For His sake, amen.

I want no other rock to build upon than that I have,
  desire no other hope than that of gospel truth,
    need no other look than that which gazes on the cross.
Forgive me if I have tried to add anything to the one founda-
tion . . .
        if I have attempted to complete what is perfect
        in Christ;
May my cry be always, Only Jesus! only Jesus!
                        —Old Puritan prayer

44

Fix your eyes on Jesus
and not on ugliness

I was sitting in the lounge of a Christian radio station, waiting my turn to go into the studio and guest a talk show. Another Christian program, on the air at that moment, was being intercommed into the lounge, so I couldn't help but listen.

It was gross.

In the name of "exposing" the sins of our day, shocking activities were being described, filthy words were being repeated. I guess listener reaction was supposed to be to pray or send money.

I thought about all the New Testament letters, written and circulated in an equally obscene world; the Roman culture was then in its last throes of degradation. But the Scriptures didn't describe the society's filth, they only warned against it; and then spent the space teaching the positive—both in doctrinal truth and practical application for daily living.

Never does Paul say Christians "need to be informed" of what they're fighting against so they can "pray intelligently." No, no! He says, "Stay ignorant!"

> Be wise about what is good, and innocent about what is evil (Romans 16:19).
> It is shameful even to mention what the disobedient do in secret (Ephesians 5:12).

How do you become "blameless and pure . . . in a crooked and perverse generation, in which you shine like stars in the universe" (Philippians 2:15)?

Philippians 4:8 tells you how:

> Whatever is true,
> whatever is noble,
> whatever is right,
> whatever is pure,
> whatever is lovely,
> whatever is admirable
>   —if anything is excellent or praiseworthy—
> think about such things.

Surrounded by ugliness, think beauty.

Fix your eyes on Jesus.

Prayer:

O Lord Jesus Christ,
John saw You among the lampstands,
    with Your face shining like the sun in all its brilliance,
    and Your voice like the sound of rushing waters,
    and seven stars in Your right hand.

I can't imagine how beautiful You must be.

A rainbow encircles You,
and before You is a sea of glass . . .
    an exquisitely pure reflecting pool . . .
      doubling all Your splendor.
I see flashes of lightening from Your throne;
    I hear exploding peals of thunder;
      I smell heavenly incense from the golden
      bowls. . . .

My senses are dazzled.

    "How handsome you are, my lover!
      Oh, how charming!'"(Song of Solomon 1:16).

Almost without breath,
    "lost in wonder, love, and praise,"
      I fix my eyes on You.

To remember Thee, to worship Thee,
to confess to Thee, to praise Thee,
to bless Thee, to hymn Thee,
to give thanks to Thee,
maker, nourisher, guardian, governor,
preserver, worker, perfector of all,
Lord and Father,
King and God,
fountain of life and immortality,
treasure of everlasting goods,
whom the heavens hymn,
and the heaven of heavens,
the angels and all the heavenly powers,
one to another crying continually—
and we the while, weak and unworthy,
under their feet—

> *Holy, Holy, Holy,*
> *Lord God of Hosts;*
> *full is the whole heaven,*
> *and the whole earth,*
> *of the majesty of Thy glory. . . .*

---

*Fragment of the private written devotions of Lancelot Andrewes (1555–1626), chaplain to Queen Elizabeth I and one of the translators of the 1611 King James Version of the Bible.

45

Fix your eyes on Jesus only

"One's ultimate loyalty must converge at a single point. To try to go two ways at once will rip a person down the middle."

(Vernard Eller)

Jesus to Martha: "Only one thing is necessary"

(Luke 10:42).

"What is that one thing? Surely it is that God be loved and praised for Himself above all other occupations of the body or soul."

(*The Cloud of Unknowing*)

> . . . Thee will I cherish,
> Thee will I honor,
> Thou, my soul's glory, joy andcrown!
>   ("Fairest Lord Jesus," 17th century)

"The secret of successful Christians has been that they had a sweet madness for Jesus about them."
        (A.W. Tozer)

Jesus Christ is Square One, and anything not related to Him is ultimately meaningless and futile.

"Believers may not often realize it, but even as believers we are either centered on God or centered on man.

"There is no alternative. Either God has become the center of our universe and we have become rightly adjusted to Him, or we have made ourselves the center, and are attempting to make everything else orbit around us and for us."
        (Paul Fromke)

Dr. Henry Drummond to his theological students: "Don't touch Christianity unless you plan to make Him first. If you put Him second, I promise you a miserable existence."

> Were I possessor of the earth
>   And call'd the stars my own,
> Without Thy graces and Thyself
>   I were a wretch undone.

Let others stretch their arms like seas
And grasp in all the shore:
Grant me the visits of Thy face,
And I desire no more."[1]

"Lord, Thou hast made us for Thyself, and our hearts are restless until they rest in Thee."

(St. Augustine, first century)

"Every day I see again that only You can teach me to pray, only You can set my heart at rest, only You can let me dwell in Your presence.

"No book, no idea, no concept or theory will ever bring me close to You unless You Yourself are the One who lets these instruments become the way to You."

(Henri J.M. Nouwen)

"I lift up my eyes to you, to you whose throne is in heaven."

(Psalm 123:1)

"As to other gods I am an atheist, but as to God the Son Who came forth from Him and taught us these things, I worship and adore Him."

(Justin Martyr, first century)

Glorious God,
It is the flame of my life to worship thee,
the crown and glory of my soul to adore thee,
heavenly pleasure to approach.

(Old Puritan prayer)

"I am A and Z, the First and Last!"

(Jesus Christ, Revelation 1:11, TLB)

"Lift up your heart unto God, then, with a meek and long-
ing love; let there be but a naked intent unto God alone."

(*The Cloud of Unknowing*)

None other Lamb, none other Name,
    None other Hope in heaven or earth or sea,
None other Hiding Place from guilt and shame—
    None beside Thee!

(Christina Rossetti, 1830–1894)

---

[1] (I copied this 1827 poem as I saw it embroidered, framed, and hanging on a wall of Crathes Castle in northern Scotland.)

Quotations above: Vernard Eller from *The Simple Life*, p. 24. "What is that one thing," etc.: *The Cloud of Unknowing*, p. 75. Fragment of hymn "Fairest Lord Jesus," from *Gesangbuch*, Münster, 1677; tr. anonymous 1850. Henri Nouwen from Job and Shawchuck's *A Guide to Prayer*, p. 119; quotation from Nouwen's *A Cry for Mercy*.

46

Fix your eyes on Jesus right now

"My eyes are fixed on you, O Sovereign Lord."

(Psalm 141:8)

> Calvin Coolidge: "We cannot do everything at once, but we can do *something* at once."

Pray your own prayer to Him.

I'm praying this will be a book not just for you to *read* but to *do*! I would love to hear how you have fixed your eyes on Jesus anew.

Love,

Anne Ortlund
32 Whitewater Drive
Corona del Mar
California 92625
U.S.A.

BIBLIOGRAPHY

Buechner, Frederick, *The Faces of Jesus* (Riverwood Publ., 1974; Stearn/ Harper and Row, 1989).

Cloud of Unknowing, The, a version in modern English of a fourteenth-century classic (N.Y.: Harper and Bros., 1948).

Dods, Marcus, *Christ and Man* (London: Hodder and Stoughton, 1909).

Eller, Vernard, *The Simple Life* (Grand Rapids: Wm. B. Eerdmans Publ., 1973).

Frances de Sales, *Introduction to a Devout Life* (Cleveland, N.Y.: World Publ. Co., 1952).

Gold Dust, Charlotte Yonge, ed. (N.Y.: Grosset and Dunlap, 1900, 1903).

Harton, F.P., *The Elements of the Spiritual Life* (London: S.P.C.K., Holy Trinity Church, 1932, 1964).

Hession, Roy and Revel, *We Would See Jesus* (Fort Washington, PA: Christian Literature Crusade, Publ., 1958).

Hopkins, Evan, "Threefold Delivery," message printed in *Keswick's Authentic Voice,* Herbert F. Stevenson, ed. (London: Marshall, Morgan and Scott, 1959).

Job, Reuben P., and Norman Shawchuck, *A Guide to Prayer* (Nashville: The Upper Room Publ., 1983).

Keswick Week, 1955, The (London: Marshall, Morgan and Scott, 1955).

King, Guy H., *Brought In* (London: Marshall, Morgan and Scott, 1949).

Lancelot Andrewe's Private Devotions (Cleveland, N.Y. : World Publ. Co., 1956).

Law, William, *A Serious Call to a Devout and Holy Life* (Philadelphia: Westminster Press, 1948).

Lewis, C.S., *The Screwtape Letters.*

Maclaren, Alexander, *Christ in the Heart* (N.Y.: Funk and Wagnalis Publ., 1905).

Monod, Theodore, *Looking unto Jesus* (pamphlet tr. French to English by Helen Willis, printed in Hong Kong, 1957).

Murray, Andrew, *Abide in Christ* (N.Y.: Grosset and Dunlap, undated).

Murray, Andrew, *Like Christ* (N.J.: Fleming H. Revell, 1895)

Ortlund, Anne, *Discipling One Another* (Dallas: Word Books, 1979).

Ortlund, Anne, *Up with Worship* (Ventura, CA: Regal Books, 1975, 1982).

Ortlund, Raymond C., *Lord, Make My Life a Miracle* (Ventura, CA: Regal Books, 1974).

Pocket William Law, The, excerpts of writings c. 1750, Arthur W. Hopkinson, ed. (London: Latimer House Ltd., 1950).

Sanders, Oswald J., *Christ Incomparable* (Fort Washington, PA: Christian Literature Crusade Publ., 1952).

Still Waters, Deep Waters, Rowland Croucher, ed. (Sydney: Albatross Books, 1987).

Tozer, A.W., *The Pursuit of God* (Harrisburg, PA: Christian Publications, 1948).

Valley of Vision, The, Arthur Bennett, ed. (Edinburgh: "The Banner of Truth Trust," 1975).

STUDY GUIDE
FOR GROUP USE

SESSION 1: Chapters 1–2

1. Chapter 1: Describe in your own words the salvation process, whereby God is on one side and man on the other, and Christ bringing us to God. When and how did you come to Him?

2. Chapter 2: *A frank admission of need* is always God's "ticket of admission" to His solutions. Do you see anything on the list on page 9 that you need to be saved from? Do you want to add others?

3. Read Hebrews 12: 1–3, and spend time in group prayer that this study may meet your personal needs and direct your life focuses truly to Jesus.

To prepare for Session 2, let each member of the group pick one or two chapters between 3 and 14 with which he/she can identify, and be ready to report on those chapters, hopefully with personal applications.

SESSION 2: Chapters 3–14, to get practical help

Bring a kitchen timer clock to help monitor the timing of the reports on chapters 3 to 14! (Have some fun with this, but still try to keep on schedule.)

Then spend time in prayer for specific solutions to those areas of need.

Similarly, to prepare for Session 3, let each member of the group pick one or two chapters between 15 and 24 with which he/she can identify, and be ready to report on those chapters, hopefully with personal applications.

SESSION 3: Chapters 15–24, to reshape your life

Bring the kitchen timer clock again, to help monitor the timing of the reports on chapters 15 to 24!

Then spend time in prayer for specific solutions to those areas of need.

SESSION 4: Chapter 26, Jesus as seen in the Bible

1. Pages 129 and 130: Have members of the group read John 5:39 and Luke 24:25–27, 44, 45. Then let several pray that our minds may be open to understand Christ in the Scriptures.

Together look at each of the passages quoted here in Chapter 26, putting one finger in the Old Testament quotation and another finger in the New Testament identification of Christ. Think how, over a span of so many centuries, God bound His book together by the person of His Son!

Can you name other New Testament passages that identify Jesus in the Old Testament? (For instance, there are at least 11 in the Gospel of Matthew.)

2.a. On pages 132 and 133, when you see descriptions of yourself in the New Testament verses, what descriptions do you see that need particular prayer and obedience to be fulfilled in you?

b. How can you help each other in the group attain these characteristics, by specific intercessory prayer and accountability? Do some strategizing!

Pray together in unison the verses in the Psalms quoted in the chapter's closing prayer. Continue praying your own prayers in the light of these.

SESSION 5: Chapters 27 and 28, Son of Man and Son of God

1. Read through these two chapters looking up each Scripture verse mentioned and reading it in full.

2. Read Philippians 2:5–11.
    a. Which descriptions allude to Christ's being fully man? Which descriptions allude to His being fully God?
    b. What difference should it make in your attitude and personality to obey verse 5?

3. Read all of Colossians 1: 13–20, partially quoted on page 143. Describe all that you see here of various facets of Jesus Christ.

4. Read the poems between and following these two chapters; spend time in group prayer worshiping Him for being the perfect God Man.

SESSION 6: Chapters 29–31, Jesus the Messiah, crucified, risen

1. Chapter 29, *Jesus the Messiah*
    a. How do you describe a prophet?
      a priest?
      a king?
    b. How was Jesus a double prophet?
      How was He a double priest?
      How was He a double king?
    c. How does He perform each of these functions in your life?

2. Chapter 30, *Jesus crucified*
Read Joshua 20: 1–6, a wonderful provision for Old Testament justice.
    How does this situation picture Jesus as the innocent victim?
    How does it also picture Him as our place of refuge?

3. Chapter 31, *Jesus risen*
Were you personally most struck by the risen Christ's provision of presence, peace, purpose or power? Why?

Spend a time in prayers of thanksgiving for all these aspects of Jesus.

*SESSION 7: Chapters 32–34, Jesus the Eternal One, coming again,
and on nothing else clearly*

1. Chapter 32, *Jesus the Eternal One*
Jesus says in John 14:2 that He is preparing a place for us.
How do the following references which mention a "place"
help to describe what that place might be like?
    Exodus 3:5, Joshua 5:15
    Psalm 26:8
    Psalm 32:7
    Isaiah 66:1

2. Chapter 33, *Jesus coming again*
First John 2:28 says we prepare for Jesus' coming by *abiding
in Him*. Practically, how can we do that, to make sure we're ready
for Him?

3. Chapter 34, *on Jesus and on nothing else clearly*
If Hebrews 12:2 says to look *away* to Jesus, what do you
think of in your own life that you need to *look away from*, to see
Him more clearly?
Spend a time of prayer asking Him that you may do this—
to focus off of specific things in order to focus on Him.
To prepare for Session 8, let each member of the group pick
one or two chapters between 35 and 44 of particular personal
interest, and be ready to report on those chapters, hopefully with
personal applications.

SESSION 8: Chapters 35–44, to get focus

Bring back that kitchen timer clock to help monitor the
timing of the reports on chapters 35 to 44!
Then spend time in prayer for specific applications.

To get ready for Session 9, let each member of the group prepare to report on any parts of the book he/she feels got slighted.

SESSION 9: Wrap-up and worship

Include the kitchen timer clock again! And let the reports conclude 15 to 20 minutes before closing time.

Finish with group worship:

1. Read in unison the prayer on pages 211 and 212, and follow it with Lancelot Andrewe's prayer on page 213, also in unison.

2. If you know them or have song books, sing hymns and songs about Christ's holiness.

3. Perhaps on your knees, be in prayerful worship as members of the group volunteer to read to the Lord favorite quotations of chapter 45, in any order.

4. Continue with free worship in prayer, adoring Him, describing Him back to Himself, quoting Scriptures about Him, or breaking into worship songs.

5. Conclude, if you know it, by singing the Doxology.

Other Books by the Ortlunds

Anne Ortlund, *Up With Worship*, Regal Books (what should happen between your ears on a Sunday morning)

Anne Ortlund, *Disciplines of the Beautiful Woman*, Word Books (life management through a notebook, desk wardrobe, etc)

Anne Ortlund, *Discipling One Another*, Word Books ("how to's" for small fellowship groups)

Anne Ortlund, *Children Are Wet Cement*, Fleming H. Revell (handling children; Christy Award for best marriage-family book of 1982)

Anne Ortlund, *Joanna: A Story of Renewal*, Word Books (Anne's first fiction)

Anne Ortlund, *Building A Great Marriage*, Fleming H. Revell (for any age but especially early marriage)

Anne Ortlund, *Disciplines of the Heart*, Word Books (on a woman's inner life)

Anne Ortlund, *Disciplines of the Home*, Word Books (on family life together)

Raymond C. and Anne Ortlund, *The Best Half of Life*, Word Books (from age 35 on: money, marriage, goals, etc.)

Raymond C. and Anne Ortlund, *You Don't Have to Quit*, Oliver-Nelson (perseverance in marriage, job, school, relationships, etc.)

Raymond C. and Anne Ortlund, *Confident in Christ*, Multnomah (what it means to be in Christ; its privileges, its responsibilities)

Raymond C. and Anne Ortlund, *Renewal*, NavPress (a study guide on the three priorities, for group use)

Raymond C. Ortlund, *Be a New Christian All Your Life*, Fleming H. Revell (for new Christians or those who want to be renewed)

Raymond C. Ortlund, *Intersections*, Word Books (studies in the Gospel of Luke)

Raymond C. Ortlund, *Three Priorities for a Strong Local Church*, Word Books (for pastors and lay leaders)

Raymond C. Ortlund, *Lord, Make My Life a Miracle*, Regal Books (priorites to live by)